Working With Bere...

Working With Bereavement

A Practical Guide

Janet Wilson

palgrave
macmillan

First published 2014 by
PALGRAVE MACMILLAN

Palgrave Macmillan in the UK is an imprint of Macmillan Publishers
Limited, registered in England, company number 785998, of Hound-
mills, Basingstoke, Hampshire RG21 6XS.

Palgrave Macmillan in the US is a division of St Martin's Press LLC,
175 Fifth Avenue, New York, NY 10010.

Palgrave Macmillan is the global academic imprint of the above
companies and has companies and representatives throughout the
world.

Palgrave® and Macmillan® are registered trademarks in the United
States, the United Kingdom, Europe and other countries

ISBN: 978-0-230-29145-4

This book is printed on paper suitable for recycling and made from
fully managed and sustained forest sources. Logging, pulping and
manufacturing processes are expected to conform to the environmental regulations of the country of origin.

A catalogue record for this book is available from the British Library.

A catalog record for this book is available from the Library of
Congress.

Printed in China.

To my parents who taught
me much through their lives.

Contents

List of Figures and Tables

Figures

Tables

Acknowledgements

I am grateful to Colin Feltham for initially suggesting I write this book and helping to prepare the proposal and to Melanie Gee who created the index. Thanks to Palgrave Macmillan particularly Catherine Gray and India Annette-Woodgate for their ongoing advice and support while writing. I am also thankful to friends and colleagues who have supported me as I wrote the various chapters. *Speak encouraging words to one another* (1Thess 5v11). Special thanks go to the many people who have shared their experiences of bereavement with me.

The authors and publisher would like to thank the following publishers and organizations for permission to reproduce copyright material:

Cengage Learning for their permission to reproduce and adapt 'The Whirlpool of Grief' from Bob Spall and Stephen Callis, *Loss, Bereavement and Grief: A guide to effective caring* (1997).

Taylor and Francis Ltd. for their permission to reproduce 'The Dual Process Model' from Margaret Stroebe and Henk Schut, 'The Dual Process Model of Coping with Bereavement: Rationale and Descriptions' in *Death Studies*, 23:3 197–224 (1999).

Introduction

Health and social care practitioners and others involved in caring for and supporting people are likely at some time in their work to encounter people who are bereaved by the death of someone close to them. In the United Kingdom for example people are reluctant to talk about death (Kirshbaum, 2011). Many people feel awkward around the subject of death and try to avoid contact with a recently bereaved person for fear of upsetting them or not knowing what to say. There are frequent reports from those who are bereaved that friends and neighbours appear to actively avoid coming into contact with them, which results in them feeling isolated. Another issue often raised is that friends and relatives expect the grieving person to be back to what they consider to be their normal self within a few weeks of the death. When someone close to a person dies life will never be the same again for the bereaved person. It will take time for them to adjust and learn to live without the person who has died, and this can be a very varied period of time

The aim of this book is to provide both factual information and advice for those working with the bereaved, whether the death is very recent or many years ago. I have included topics and issues of which I have knowledge and experience and which have resulted in questions of what to do in certain circumstances or situations.

Working with bereavement can be emotionally draining and you need to have an awareness of your own coping strategies, how you deal with stress and what is constructive and helpful for you in this work. The final chapter of this book considers this important aspect of self-care.

Terms used in the book

Practitioner. This term is used to refer to anyone having the role of supporting a bereaved person. It can include a wide range of people from diverse backgrounds including nurses, healthcare assistants, hospice staff, physiotherapists, occupational therapists, chaplains, social workers, counsellors, volunteers and students undertaking health and social care courses. In particular situations, specific staff groups may be referred to such as hospice staff or nurses but generally the term practitioner is used to indicate that this could include a range of people.

Client: This term is used to identify the person who is bereaved. It is often used to refer to the person being supported in a counselling setting, however, here it is also used to include patients and service users.

Applied examples: Throughout the book there are examples used to illustrate issues and situations that can arise. They are based on my own experiences and knowledge and names, circumstances and identifying features have been altered so bear little similarity to actual situations and individuals encountered. Any perceived similarity is therefore entirely coincidental and in no way intentional

'Over to you'/Reflection: These are suggestions of times when you may want to consider an issue for yourself or reflect on your own experiences or thoughts of a particular issue or topic.

A note about myself

I am a nurse so many of the sources used in this book are from my nursing knowledge and experience. I have also worked as a volunteer in a charity supporting those who are bereaved and am a psychotherapist, so experiences from these settings are also included.

The book's structure

There are nine chapters each concentrating on specific aspects of bereavement.

● Chapter 1: Different theories and models of bereavement are used to explain how people respond following a death and factors that may help people to understand and manage their grief.

- Chapter 2: The importance of communication skills is explained with sections on support: pre-bereavement, at the time of death and following the death. Working creatively is also covered in this chapter
- Chapter 3: The different approaches and types of support are discussed, along with the physical environment and professional issues such as confidentiality and boundaries.
- Chapter 4: Cultural and faith influences and how these may affect the grieving process, along with examples of practices from a range of belief traditions.
- Chapter 5: How different aspects such as age and relationship can affect bereavement. This chapter also explores the responses seen to celebrity deaths, the increasing presence of roadside memorials and the debate concerning the medicalization of grief.
- Chapter 6: A range of sudden and traumatic deaths are explored including road traffic collisions, military deaths, murder and major disasters.
- Chapter 7: Deaths which are not commonly talked about including suicide and the death of a baby or child.
- Chapter 8: Unrecognized grief is discussed, explaining the concept of disenfranchised particularly in relation to a bereaved person with learning disabilities, and those bereaved through a person having dementia or HIV/AIDS.
- Chapter 9: The very important aspect of self-care for the practitioner, explaining why this is needed and suggestions of how to care for yourself.

1 Theories of Bereavement

Introduction

The words, bereavement, grief and mourning are often used interchangeably in relation to death, however, there are distinctive differences in the meanings of these words. Bereavement is the word used to describe the death of someone. A bereaved person is one who has experienced the death of someone close to them. This term is also used more generally to refer to other losses a person experiences in life of things that are important to them. This can be the loss of a job, home, relationship or other aspect of life. Grief is the emotional response to the death, the thoughts, feelings and behaviours a person has as a result of the death. It can include a range of responses including sadness, anger, crying and withdrawal. Mourning involves the actions a person carries out following a death. These can be individual and are often collective and based on cultural and belief systems in terms of the type of funeral and attendance at other events such as a wake, wearing certain clothes and adhering to rituals. Actions can include staying at home for a certain time, not attending social events and dressing in certain colours, or clothing, to identify to others that they are in mourning.

When a person dies it is recognized that there are responses from those known to them. This includes the psychological, biological and sociological aspects of loss and covers a range of issues such as physical, cognitive, behavioural and spiritual aspects of grief (Parkes, 1975). Throughout the twentieth century and into the twenty-first century there have been many theories and views of bereavement and how people may respond when someone close to them dies. Some of these theories have been very specific and looked at the distinct journey or route people are thought to take through grief. A few of these theories may seem prescriptive and they try to fit a person's response to death into a set of fixed behaviours and feelings. Most of the theories acknowledge that individuals differ and allow for flexibility in responses but this is not always recognized. Some theories actually seem to contradict others and over time ideas and understandings of responses to death and what may be helpful have developed and changed. This chapter contains details of some of the theories of bereavement ranging from Freud (1917) to the present day.

Every individual that experiences bereavement will bring to the situation their past experiences in life, influences from their social and cultural background and their own attitudes and values. All these will impact on how they respond to the death (Katz and Johnson, 2006). Some will have had previous experiences of bereavement and this is likely to influence how they manage their emotions following subsequent deaths.

Freud: mourning and melancholia

Sigmund Freud is well known for his work describing the effects of the conscious and unconscious mind. The conscious mind according to Freud is that which we are aware of at any particular moment including perceptions, memories, thoughts, feelings and fantasies. The unconscious mind includes things not easily available to our awareness such as drives, instincts, memories and emotions associated with past trauma. In his writing on mourning and melancholia Freud stated that mourning is a reaction to the loss of a loved person. It involves a painful frame of mind, loss of both an interest in the outside world and loss of a capacity to adopt any new object of love. The person in mourning also turns away from any activity not connected with thoughts of the dead person (Freud, 1949).

Freud continues that although mourning involves a departure from what are considered normal attitudes to life it is not regarded as a pathological condition. It does not require referral for medical treatment. Freud concluded that individuals overcome the state of mourning themselves after a period of time and that interference with the process is useless and could even be harmful.

Melancholia is viewed by Freud as including all the symptoms associated with grief with the addition of a feeling of low self-worth. The person sees themselves as worthless, incapable of any achievement, and expects to be cast out and punished by those around them. Melancholia can result from the death of a loved one or from the loss of an object or a relationship. The person may be aware of who they have lost but not what they have lost in that person. The person who has died may have been their companion giving emotional support or provided a practical service such as the manager of their finances. Freud's view was that in melancholia the individual may not be consciously aware of the specific object or feature that has been lost, whereas in mourning, the loss is totally within the conscious mind of the individual.

Freud viewed the personality of an individual as comprising of three parts, the ego, superego and the id. The id he saw as the instincts, wishes and impulses an individual has, the ego as the rational, decision making, logical part enabling a person to distinguish between a wish and reality and the superego as the conscience, judging and representing the internalization of parental and moral values (Gross, 2005). In melancholia Freud believed it was the ego that was affected.

Mourning is a natural process and frees the participant upon its completion. It travels a cycle of adjustment, and a form of rebirth occurs as the bereaved person disengages from the dead person, and re-engages with life to live without the loved one who has died.

Melancholia remains an unnatural open wound that continues within a cycle. There is no detachment from the person who has died or attachment to others that are alive and therefore no moving on to re-engage with life. Melancholia as defined by Freud is an illness requiring treatment.

Lindemann: acute grief and rituals

Eric Lindemann was a psychiatrist who coined the phrase 'acute grief' to describe what happens to people when a loved one dies. His study involved people who were survivors of a fire that spread through a nightclub in Boston in 1942 killing 492 people (Lindemann, 1944). He wrote about the importance of rituals surrounding deaths such as funerals, memorials and of group mourning.

As a result of his study Lindemann described grief as being remarkably uniform comprising a common range of symptoms, including:

● Physical (somatic) symptoms: tightness of the throat, choking, shortness of breath, an empty feeling in the stomach, tension.
● Pre-occupation with the deceased: hallucinations, seeing or sensing the deceased's presence, a sense of unreality.
● Guilt.
● Hostility.
● Changes in behaviour: restless, aimless, loss of concentration.
● Identification with the deceased; assuming traits of the deceased, showing signs of illness of the deceased.

Kübler-Ross: stages of loss

Elizabeth Kübler-Ross worked as a psychiatrist with those who were dying, mostly in a hospice setting. Through this work she identified five stages that terminally ill patients experience. These were denial, anger, bargaining, depression and acceptance. She went on to apply these stages to those who were bereaved (Kübler-Ross, 1973). Below are details of each of the five stages and how they are applied by Kübler-Ross to the terminally ill and to the bereaved.

1. Denial and isolation

For the terminally ill – the diagnosis must be wrong, it is not them who have this illness, it happens to others but not them

For the bereaved – it cannot be their loved one who has died, it must be someone else. The viewing of the body can help people to acknowledge that the death is real and it is their loved one who has died and not someone else. When there is no body it can be very difficult for the bereaved to accept what has happened

2. Anger

For the terminally ill – questioning, why is it happening to me? What have I done to deserve this?

For the bereaved – often aimed at health professionals, family members, work and society. The bereaved person can be very irrational and it can be difficult to deal with someone who is angry in this way. With some, the anger can progress to complaints being made to the hospital, workplace, school, and so forth.

3. Bargaining

For the terminally ill – promising to do anything as long as they can live, that they will live a good life, behave in certain way, give their money away, for example.

For the bereaved – they may try to bargain with God or another higher power they perceive to be in charge of the world. They may promise to do anything as long as the person is not really dead, if they can somehow be brought back to life

4. Depression

For the terminally ill – the reality of their impending death can result in them giving up hope and falling into a deep depression

For the bereaved – they cannot see past their grief as it seems to encompass their whole life. They see no future that would be worth living.

5. Acceptance

For the terminally ill – they feel an acceptance and peace about what is happening

For the bereaved – they accept that death is part of life and that there is life for them after the death of their loved one.

They still feel the loss but are able to move on and get involved in aspects of life again.

Although this theory can be viewed as rigid, where the five stages are followed in the given order, in her writings Kübler-Ross states that people revisit the stages and so do not progress systematically from one stage to the next in sequence.

Bowlby: attachment theory

John Bowlby was a psychiatrist who developed attachment theory (1980) to describe the significance and effects of family bonds. He identified that the secure attachment of an infant to a primary carer and others in his sphere of contact is essential for children to grow up into socially competent individuals, able to trust others, achieve things and form healthy relationships. Separation causes anxiety and it is how separation is managed during childhood that determines the child's capacity for secure attachments in later life.

Adult grief is an extension of the general distress response to separation anxiety observed in young children. With children, when the parent returns the anxiety is resolved. In death there is no return so there needs to be a period of adjustment and reorganization.

Bowlby identified phases that could occur after the death of someone close. The initial phase he reported was that of numbness and disbelief, which can last for hours or weeks and may include outbursts of extreme distress and/or anger. Another phase includes yearning and searching for the deceased accompanied by anxiety and intermittent periods of anger, which can last for months or years

The bereaved person feels to be in a state of disorganization and despair. This can be accompanied by feelings of depression and apathy as old patterns are discarded. As time progresses a reorganization takes place. This results in recovery to a lesser or greater degree and acceptance of what has happened. Bowlby identified that this process, although variable, took on average a period of two years (Holmes, 1993).

Murray Parkes: phases of grief

Colin Murray Parkes worked as a psychiatrist in St Christopher's Hospice in London and has made a lifelong study of grief and bereavement. He developed a theory of phases of grief and stressed that people move around the four phases in any order repeating the phases until they have finally adjusted to living a life without the person who has died (1975). The four phases are:

1. *Shock and despair*: this involves disbelief at what has happened and a feeling of helplessness, questioning how they can possibly cope without that person.
2. *Separation and pain*: the loss is unbearable and causes pain, often both physical and emotional
3. *Acceptance*: the realization that the death really has happened; their loved one has gone forever.
4. *Resolution and reorganization*: this phase involves both an emotional and physical adjustment. Aspects of life have to change in order to be able to live and function without the person who has died.

Worden: the four tasks of mourning

William Worden, a professor of psychology states that mourning is necessary following a death. It is not a state of being but one that requires effort from the person to complete certain tasks. For Worden, grief is a process that has to be actively worked through, not a passive process that happens to an individual. His view is that it is possible to have an incomplete bereavement, just as it is possible to have incomplete healing of a physical wound. He identifies four tasks of mourning (2010) that need to be accomplished before mourning can be completed. Worden states that uncompleted grief tasks can impair further growth and development of the individual.

These tasks do not follow a specific order and there may be movement between the four tasks at certain times or in specific situations.

1. *To accept the reality of the loss*: when someone dies, even if the death is expected there can often be a sense that it hasn't really happened, it is not true that they have gone forever. Common phrases are, I can't believe she has really gone, it can't be my brother, he was fine only an hour before. The bereaved can think they see the person, hear them speak or catch a glimpse of them somewhere, and then have to remind themselves that the person really is dead.

2. *To work through the pain of grief*: not everyone experiences the same intensity of pain or feels it in the same way, but it is impossible to lose someone you have been closely attached to without experiencing some level of pain. Society can be insensitive and uncomfortable with those expressing their pain. People often feel they have to hide their emotions and pretend that they are not upset. Friends may try to take the bereaved out to get them away from thinking about their loss and its impact.

3. *Adjust to an environment in which the deceased is missing*: this process differs depending on the role the deceased had in the life of the bereaved. Different family members may approach this task in a variety of ways. It may involve learning to live alone, being a sole parent, managing finances, for example. The loss of a partner may involve multiple losses: a companion, lover, accountant, gardener, cook, baby minder.

4. *Emotionally relocate the deceased and move on with life*: this reflects the readiness of the bereaved person to involve themselves in new relationships and find an appropriate location for the deceased in their emotional lives. This task can be hindered by holding onto the past attachment rather than moving forward and forming new ones. Some people find the death of someone close so painful that they decide never to love again as they do not want to risk a repeat of this pain.

Over to you

Do you think it is useful to have a knowledge and understanding of the stages or tasks of grief from the above theories?

How might you use this knowledge when working with someone who is bereaved?

Can you identify any problems in using these theories in bereavement work?

Stroebe and Schut: dual process model

Margaret Stroebe and Henk Schut (1998, 1999) have suggested a different model to those above. They believe that some of these previous theories set up too rigid expectations of how people should grieve and can become prescriptive. They put forward a 'Dual Process Model', that focuses on the coping process and which they claim is more flexible and more sensitive to cultural differences.

Stroebe and Schut (1999) argue that you cannot neatly package grief work into stages, which need to be worked through before going on to the next stage. Their model encompasses both loss and restoration-oriented coping.

Restoration-orientated activities

- Mastering the tasks that the significant other had undertaken, for example, finances, gardening, cooking.
- Dealing with arrangements for the organization of life without the person who has died. It may be necessary to move house, change jobs or arrange childcare.
- The development of a new identity, for example, from being part of a couple to being alone. There can also be changes of title, for example, from wife, husband, daughter or son to widow, widower or orphan.
- The development of new interests and activities, for example, joining organizations and attending social events.

Loss-orientated activities

- Grief work: being upset, crying, talking about the dead person, expressing the loss and how they are missed.
- Intrusion of grief into a person's life. This can involve being reminded of the dead person by hearing a certain piece of music or being in a specific location.
- Breaking bonds and ties. This covers a range of activities and may include changing names on bank accounts and other documents, establishing different ways of doing things.

Denial and avoidance of grief appear on both sides of this model. It can be helpful to sometimes set aside grief and thoughts of the person who has died and become engaged in another activity. This may be spending time with friends, seeing a film or play or doing some other activity. It can be part of the restoration activity of establishing a new lifestyle or can be related to the loss.

In this model (see Figure 1.1) there is no set course or script and therefore there isn't the same pressure on people to be at a particular place, or stage, at a particular time or within a particular time frame

The lines that go between the loss-orientated and grief-orientated responses in Figure 1.1 illustrates how people can fluctuate between the two responses of grief, moving frequently from one to the other.

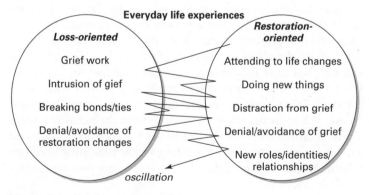

Figure 1.1 Dual process model

Source: Stroebe and Schut (1999)

This model can be useful to show to a bereaved person to help them understand what is happening to them. Often a person will relate their experiences of how they can be enjoying an activity and then suddenly become upset or be reminded unexpectedly of the dead person. They can describe how they fluctuate, often several times in one day between the different activities and do not understand what is happening to them. This diagram can help an individual to understand the process and also can normalize their experiences as they often think their experiences are unique to them and somehow not normal. Showing this diagram can demonstrate to the bereaved person that their mixed feelings are normal and can be a great relief to them.

Walter: biography

Tony Walter, a sociologist suggests that grief is more complex than one model can allow. Bereaved people generally want to talk about the deceased and through this they construct a story that places the dead person within their lives. The purpose of this is to construct a durable biography that enables the living to integrate the memory of the dead person into their ongoing life (Walter, 1996). This is achieved by talking to others, particularly those who knew the deceased. In modern society where people move frequently there may not be people around locally who knew the deceased for the bereaved person to be able to talk to. When a person dies in hospital and relatives are not present at the time, they often want to know the minute details of the person's last few hours of life. This can be what time they woke up, what they had for breakfast, what they were wearing, their conversations and who cared for them. These may seem strange questions for the bereaved to ask, but knowing these details can help the person to form a picture and a story of the last hours for their loved one and can be a comfort to them. Spending a little time with a relative informing them of these details can have a very positive impact on their grieving.

Klass, Silverman and Nickman: continuing bonds

Many of the theories already mentioned support the view that the function of grief and mourning is to cut bonds with the deceased, freeing the bereaved person to develop new relationships and move on with their lives.

In contrast, Klass, Silverman and Nickman (1996) argue that bereaved people remain involved and connected to the deceased and that continuing bonds are formed, which are important. These bonds are dynamic and change over time in a way that parallels the development of relationships with others that are still alive. Their research suggests that this feature is common, both with adults and children, though it is not always openly acknowledged. The continuing bonds people have with the bereaved enable them to maintain links with the dead person. It can involve thinking what the dead person might have done in a certain situation.

Applied example

Following a heavy frost Sam had a water pipe burst in his house. His father who had died a few years earlier was a very practical person and Sam thought "What would my father do in this situation?" He felt this helped him think through the best course of action and was comforted that he felt his father had helped him deal with this crisis even though he wasn't physically present.

Neimeyer: Reconstructing meaning

Robert Neimeyer (2001) views grief as a process of reconstructing a person's meaning of the world and their place in it. He expressed the view that people organize events in their lives by creating a story that is meaningful for them. This helps to consolidate and create an understanding of the death, what it means for the bereaved and how their life has changed as a result of the death.

A death can alter a person's views and beliefs of the world. They may have felt their life was positive and that they were in a good place. Death can shatter this view as they experience that life can also be a place where unwanted and unexpected things happen. A death can fracture a person's sense of identity and understanding of the world about them. By being supported to retell their story, the bereaved person is helped to deal with the emotional and physical loss. The person is able to reconstruct their identity, discover a new purpose or meaning in life and reorder their sense of the world.

Over to you

Can you think of a situation where you have made sense of an incident or experience by constructing a story of what happened and why?

How did it help you?

Stokes: resilience

Resilience is defined as the ability of a person to overcome obstacles such as the death of someone close to them and consists of a complex combination of personal strengths and attitudes along with interactions with family, friends and networks in their community. This community can include work colleagues, friends, neighbours and relatives. Resilience in individuals is an issue that is increasingly being studied in relation to responses to bereavement (Sandler et al., 2008; Stroebe, 2002).

Julie Stokes, a psychologist, led a project surveying almost 600 children aged 11 years and discovered a number of factors that made a positive impact on bereaved children in terms of resilience (2009).

These include:

● Peer/adult relationships: resilient children were able to make friends with other children and maintain these friendships over a period of time. They were also able to form attachments to adults and develop trust in certain people with whom they formed secure relationships.

- Emotional responses: resilient children are able to express their emotions, which could include crying and expressing anxiety, sadness, guilt and anger. They have an ability to talk about the person who has died in a way that brings comfort and value to the relationship they had with them. They are able to develop a story of the person who died and maintain a relationship with them in a healthy way. This could include remarks of 'Dad would like this', or 'What would Dad do with this?'
- Control: a resilient child has a feeling of hope for the future and an ability to look forward to what that future may have for them. They are able to establish and maintain boundaries for themselves regarding their relationships and behaviours. They feel they are in control of their own lives.
- Other factors: a supportive home environment, the ability to acknowledge their limitations and a willingness to ask for help and support.

The work on resilience by Stokes (2009) focussed on bereaved children, however, these factors can also be significant for adults. Awareness of these factors and support in developing them could assist bereaved people in developing resilience to manage their responses to death and also their responses to other traumatic or stressful situations in their lives.

Pictures and diagrams

The use of pictures and diagrams can be helpful in explaining grief to a bereaved person to help them understand what is happening. Some people can relate more readily to a diagram or picture than to an explanation or the reading of a theory.

A diagram of a solid spot can illustrate how the bereaved person's grief is the only thing they can see initially. It is as if there is nothing else in their world, the grief dominates their thoughts, feelings and view of the world. Then, as the grief process progresses, their world expands around their grief to incorporate other relationships and activities (see Figure 1.2). It is not that their grief is any less but their view of the world has enlarged to include these other aspects. This can be very helpful

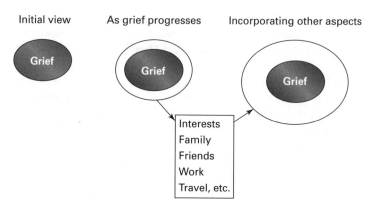

Figure 1.2 How the perception of grief can change over time

for people who may think that if they engage in other relationships or activities this will indicate that they are somehow denying how important the person, who has died, was to them and that they must maintain their level of grief to remain loyal to their loved one. This diagram shows that the grief will always be there but that other aspects are now included in their life, thus, expanding the world around their grief.

A picture many find useful is to describe grief as a waterfall (see Figure 1.3). This illustrates how a person may be progressing along the stream of life quite calmly and when someone close to them dies it is like falling over a waterfall into a whirlpool of confusion and strong emotions. The bereaved person can be washed up onto rocks of pain or the sandbanks of depression or despair. Then as they progress from the waterfall there is acceptance of the death and a reorganization of life as the person continues along the river of life on a new course.

Over to you

Can you think of situations where you might use a picture or diagram to help explain grief?

It can depend on the learning styles of individuals as to whether they find it more helpful to be told about a theory or to be

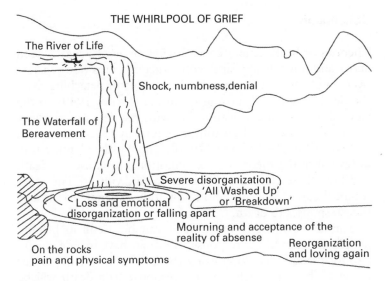

Figure 1.3 The waterfall of bereavement

Source: Spall and Callis (1997)

shown a picture or diagram. Some people relate better to an explanation or text about a topic whereas others may find a diagram more helpful in explaining their feelings. Figure 1.3, of the waterfall, can be used as an introduction to talking about grief as the bereaved person may be able to identify where they are in the picture, whether in the whirlpool, on the rocks, washed up or in the process of reorganizing their lives and adapting to a new phase of life without their loved one.

Applied example

At the first meeting of a bereavement support group for those who had experienced the death of their partner, the picture of the water-fall was given to each person. A discussion developed of the various aspects illustrated in the picture and several participants talked about where they felt they were in relation to the picture. Feedback from this group expressed the view that this was a useful way to start the group for a number of reasons. It gave members some-thing to concentrate on and hold so they were not sat looking at each other at the first meeting. It gave focus to their discussions and helped them identify their own situation. It reassured them that their feelings and experiences were recognized responses to a death.

Conclusion

Theories of bereavement cover a wide range of issues as seen above and some do appear to contradict others as views change over time. The most noticeable is the idea of detaching from the dead person and moving on in life (Freud, 1949) to the view of maintaining a relationship with the deceased through continuing bonds and creating a biography (Klass, Silverman and Nickman, 1996; Walter, 1996). There is the identification in several of the theories of the emotional responses to death and how these can vary and differ for individuals. The more recent theories concentrate on how to help people to manage their responses to death.

The above theories and models can be useful in helping people understand the responses they may have to a death and also for practitioners supporting the bereaved. It is important to remember that each person's response to a death will be unique to them and that that the models and theories are a guide to possible responses and not a prescriptive route for all to follow.

Key points

Early theories of bereavement are more prescriptive describing distinct stages of grief people experience, however, the authors do point out that stages may be revisited.

Later theories are more flexible acknowledging people fluctuate in their responses both as individuals and over time

The importance of making sense of the death, knowing details and relating the story is recognized as helping the bereaved person to adapt to life without the person who has died.

Factors that help people manage their grief and develop resilience are their abilities to: establish and maintain relationships with others; express their emotions; have hope for the future; and feel that they are in control of their lives.

Some bereaved people find it helpful to have a diagram or picture to illustrate the effect of a bereavement, others prefer an explanation or to read about theories for themselves.

Everyone's grief is unique to them as an individual, although there are common responses these vary greatly for each person and there is no set route through which every person experiencing grief travels.

Further Reading

Lewis, C.S. (1961) *A Grief Observed*. London: Faber and Faber.

Smith, H. (2004) *Griefkeeping: Learning How Long Grief Lasts*. New York: Crossroad Publishing Company.

Thompson, N. (2011) *Grief and its Challenges*. Basingstoke: Palgrave Macmillan.

Tugendhat, J. (2005) *Living with Loss and Grief*. London: Sheldon Press.

Walter, T. (1999) *On Bereavement: The Culture of Grief*. Maidenhead: Oxford University Press.

2 Working with Bereavement

Introduction

Many practitioners will have the experience of being with someone when a person they care about dies. This may be a relative or a friend of the person who has died and the death may be sudden or expected. Whatever the type of death, the bereaved person is likely to remember very clearly what is or is not said and done at the time of the death. This experience could have a profound effect on the bereaved person regarding their response to the death and their subsequent grieving.

How the practitioner responds at this time is very important.

A good death

There is considerable debate about the concept of a good death, what this means to an individual and how practitioners can support patients and their relatives in achieving this for themselves and their loved ones.

Over to you

Think of the following

● What does a good death mean to you?

● What would you like in terms of:

● Venue – where would you like to be when you die?

● Who would you like to be with you?

● Any other features you would like to be present?

Although individuals may have differing views about what would for them be a good death Addicott and Ross (2010) found for many people this would involve:

- being treated as an individual with dignity and respect;
- being without pain and other symptoms such as nausea;
- being in familiar surroundings; and
- being in the company of family or/and close friends.

The National Council for Palliative Care survey (2009) reported that about 70 per cent of people said they would prefer to die at home with their family present. However, statistics show that 60 per cent of people die in hospital (ONS, 2012). It is important to ascertain from the patient themselves, if at all possible, where they would like to die. Sometimes people change their minds as what they thought they would want may alter as they get nearer to their own death.

Applied example

Barbara had breast cancer, which had spread to her bones and lungs and knew she was going to die. She was consistently clear that she wanted to die at home and be cared for by her family and the community nursing services. She received very good care and support with well-controlled symptoms and her husband was very supportive of her decision to be at home. However, as time progressed she became anxious and felt unsafe in her own home. As a result, she requested to go to the local hospice and said she wanted to die there rather than at home. She went to the hospice and once there reported feeling relaxed and comfortable in what she viewed as a safe and secure setting. She died peacefully after spending six days in the hospice.

It is important to be open to patients changing their views on where to die. Some may be in a hospital and be desperate to go home so they can die in familiar surroundings with their family present. Sadly it sometimes takes a long time for arrangements regarding services and equipment to be put in place at a person's home. This can result in the person dying in hospital while still waiting to go home.

Death is a unique event in each person's life, we only do it once and it is important that healthcare professionals do everything possible to ensure it is the best it possibly can be for every individual person. The last thing healthcare professionals can do for a person is to care for them at their time of death and immediately afterwards. This is both a privilege and a responsibility to ensure that the person has a good death, whatever that means for them, that bereaved relatives are appropriately supported, that everyone involved is treated with compassion and dignity and that communication is clear and explicit.

Most complaints in healthcare are concerned with issues around communication. This results from people feeling they are not clearly informed of what is happening, they cannot get to talk to people concerned with their own or their relative's care or they are not listened to when they have problems or issues relating to their illness (Parliamentary and Health Service Ombudsman, 2013).

Appropriate and supportive communication around the time of death for the person dying and the bereaved relatives can have a very positive effect on the bereaved, resulting in them feeling valued and cared for themselves by the professionals they encounter. What is considered a good death experience for the person dying and their relatives can vary greatly. Each situation around death and each individual are unique. Staff must use their sensitivity and knowledge of the people concerned in assessing how to respond.

Communication skills

Communication is a vital skill for all those working in health and social care. It is a complex interaction and includes not just what we say, but how we say it, our body language and behaviour. Verbal communication can include specific words or phrases we commonly use and figures of speech. It can also include accents and the tone of our voice and fluency. How we feel about ourselves can also impact on how we communicate with others. Whether we are anxious, confident, fearful, uncertain or angry can all be communicated without using words and affect how we interact with others

Non-verbal communication includes eye contact, whether we look at the other person and how frequently. Other non-verbal forms of communication are arm and hand movements, facial expressions, body posture, touch and personal space (how close or distant we are from the person with whom we are communicating). Dress in terms of clothes, absence or presence of a uniform, piercings, hair, make-up, tattoos and so on can also communicate to others about who we are and may indicate our values and beliefs.

Over to you

Make a list of the functions of non-verbal communication

It is impossible to not communicate with others. Even if we refuse to say anything or to look at another person, by doing these things we are still communicating something to the recipient.

The functions of non-verbal communication involve being a replacement for, or accompanying and supporting, speech, and expressing emotions. It can also involve performing rituals.

There are barriers to communication and these can involve a range of factors. Age and gender can be a barrier for some in terms of people feeling comfortable talking to others. Language can be an issue in a range of areas. If a person has a strong regional accent, uses local phrases not widely understood, or does not speak the language of the other person then these can be major barriers. In health and social care, practitioners can use terms and abbreviations specific to their area of work, which are not understood by those not familiar with health or social care work. It is important to relate to people on an appropriate level, not talking down to or patronizing someone by using simplistic language but not assuming a knowledge and understanding that is not present. Clients and patients can be reluctant to say they do not understand what they are told and it is the responsibility of the practitioner to check the existing knowledge base and understanding of the person they are speaking to. This can be carried out by asking the person what their current understanding of the situation is and then developing the conversation to provide extra knowledge and information.

We need to develop an awareness of how we relate to others, what our strengths are and what areas we need to further develop. We can do this by being aware of how people respond to us, how comfortable we feel talking to people in a range of situations and reflecting on these experiences.

Over to you

Think of three different experiences you have had of communicating over the past week. These could be with friends, at work, in a social setting, with strangers or family members.

Make a list of what went well in these interactions and what you would like to improve or change if in a similar situation in the future

---

In communicating with others we need to engage in active listening. This means paying attention not only to the words that are being used, but the tone, volume and manner in which they are said and the body language used by the speaker. Listening is not a passive activity but requires the use of our visual senses as well and is something that takes great concentration.

In communicating with people in a health or social care setting there are recognized principles that Carl Rogers (2002), who developed the concept of person-centred counselling, called core conditions. These include empathy, congruence and unconditional positive regard (Donnelly and Neville, 2008).

Empathy is the ability to have some insight into what the other person is experiencing in their situation. It is not possible to fully know what another person is experiencing, as everyone responds in different ways to an experience, but by paying attention and listening actively to another person we can gain some insight into what it may be like to see the world as they do in terms of their situation. Empathy is sometimes confused with sympathy, which is feeling sorry for someone and showing you care for them, but this is different from empathy.

Congruence means being real with the person, genuineness is another word commonly used to describe this feature. It means that we say what we really mean and not things that are false, or that our body language and the words we use do not match. If a person says they are concerned for us but are constantly looking at their watch or not paying attention to what we say then we are not likely to believe their words as their speech is not congruent with their behaviour.

Unconditional positive regard means that we do not judge people for their behaviours, attitudes, values or beliefs, that we accept them as they are. People can quickly pick up if they are being judged or they are been viewed negatively, even if no words are used to indicate this.

These core conditions require us to be aware of how we appear to others in the areas of both verbal and non-verbal communication. Communication is a skill we are continually developing and adapting to the individual situations we encounter and are fundamental to being an effective practitioner.

Pre-bereavement support

This phrase is used to describe the support given to relatives and others prior to the terminally ill person's death. Although it is never possible to say precisely when a person will die, there are some conditions in which the course of the illness and the likelihood of the time of death is able to be determined to a large extent. The trajectory of dying was first described by Glaser and Strauss (1965) and refers to the rate of motion and length of progression from a life threatening illness to death. With certain cancers there is a steady decline in the person's health until death occurs and this time can be estimated from the known information of people who have died from that particular cancer in the past. With other terminal illnesses such as chronic lung or heart disease the trajectory can be much more unpredictable. People with these illnesses can have several acute exacerbations of their condition and then recover, before they die from an episode of their illness. This makes the trajectory of death much harder to predict.

Research by Metzger and Gray (2008) has identified the benefits of pre-bereavement support from practitioners. These researchers found in their study on pre-bereavement communication that individuals who begin to accept and understand the impending death of their loved one have better outcomes in terms of managing their grief after the death. Reid et al. (2006) discovered that how patients and relatives were treated during the final stages of the patient's terminal illness had a significant influence upon their experience of bereavement.

In working with relatives pre-bereavement it is important that the patient is in a state of knowing regarding what is happening and also to check whether they are in agreement with information being shared with relatives or others close to them.

It is increasingly recognized that it is important for family members to be given honest information to enable them to plan for their remaining time with their relative and prepare for the impending death (Payne et al., 2004).

This time can be used to enable both the patient and relatives to share important things they want to say to each other and may also involve the planning of the funeral service. It can be very comforting for families, to know they have carried out the wishes of the person who has died.

Applied example

Jean was 84 with lung cancer and was told she had only about three months to live. She had a husband, three children and five grandchildren whose ages ranged from 7 to 11years. Together with her family she planned her funeral service, including choosing hymns and readings and where she would like to be buried. The grandchildren were included in the discussions and the family spent much time together in those three months, sharing their lives. After the death the family were very grateful for the times they had spent together prior to the death, being able to say, to Jean, what they really wanted to and also knowing that they had carried out her wishes regarding her funeral service and burial.

At the time of death

The time, setting and place of death can all have the potential to impact on both the relatives and the practitioners caring for the person who dies. The significance of the moment of death can be viewed from several perspectives. When it is recognized that a person has died practitioners may think they have to say something, to fill a silence and somehow make it alright for the person who is bereaved. Sometimes just to be present is all that is needed. The account below describes a daughter's experience when her father died.

Applied example

When my father died, two healthcare workers were present in the room. They both stood quietly for a few minutes as I stood silently by the bed. They then asked if I wanted to be left alone with my father. In response to my reply they silently retreated so I could have some time alone with him. I found these staff very respectful and sensitive. They were present but not intrusive and showed great sensitivity. In contrast a doctor was also present who had never seen my father before. When he died she started saying he had been ill for a long time and it was to be expected. I knew all this better than she did, as I knew she had no knowledge of my father prior to this time. I experienced her words as insincere and patronizing. I would have preferred it if she had said nothing.

The example illustrates how being silent and sensitive can be appreciated and that it can be better to say nothing than to try to offer an explanation when you do not know the situation or have a relationship with either the deceased or the relative.

Although there are not specific phrases and words to say when someone dies there are general principles that can be used to guide your actions.

Some relatives may want time alone with the person who has died. It may be necessary to straighten the person in the bed and lay them flat. This can be done with the relatives present or sometimes relatives may wish to leave the room while this is carried out.

Relatives can then be left alone with the person who has died or they may wish a nurse or other healthcare worker to stay with them. Staff can be unsure whether the relatives want to be left alone so it is always wise to check what they would prefer.

Relatives could have questions that may relate to the illness or to practical issues of what happens now regarding the death certificate and funeral arrangements. It is ideal if someone who knows the patient and the family is available to answer these.

Questions about practical issues can vary depending on the place of death and what thoughts the relatives have, if any, regarding the undertaker, for example. Most hospitals and hospices have a bereavement officer who can advise and support relatives in these practical matters. If the death is at home, the doctor or nursing services can also put relatives in touch with bereavement services. Funeral directors can be very helpful in supporting relatives through the process of arranging the funeral, including advice on registering the death and other practical issues.

In hospitals the care given to a patient after death has been traditionally referred to as 'last offices'. This phrase can have both military and religious associations and can refer solely to the preparation of the body prior to removal to the mortuary. The term "care after death" has been introduced by the National End of Life Care programme and National Nurse Consultant Group (Palliative care) in their document called *Guidance for Staff Responsible for Care after Death* (2011). This phrase is intended to include a range of caring tasks required at this time, including the ongoing support of family and carers as well as the physical preparation of the body.

Providing this type of care requires sensitive and skilled communication, addressing the needs of family members and respecting the integrity of the person who has died. It can be a very emotionally challenging time for those who have been bereaved and also for the carers who may have formed relationships with both the person who has died and their family. Care after death involves a range of aspects.

Preparation of the body for transfer to a mortuary or funeral directors, usually involves washing the person and dressing them in either night clothes or a shroud. Family members may want to be involved in this process and should be supported by care staff in this. People from certain cultures and faiths may want others from their own community to carry out this procedure and this can be arranged in negotiation with the family.

Ensuring the health and safety of everyone who comes into contact with the body is important. Body fluids can be a potential source of infection so it should be ensured that both care staff and any family members involved are protected from contact with body fluids from the person who has died. Alongside this it must be ensured that the privacy and dignity of the deceased person is maintained at all times.

Respecting the cultural and spiritual wishes of the person who has died and their families, while ensuring legal obligations are met. Some cultures and faiths may want the person buried or cremated within 24 hours of their death. However, if the death has been unexpected there may be the legal requirement of a post mortem, which is likely to delay the funeral. This can be distressing for the family and requires great sensitivity from practitioners involved in this situation. In 2013 a system was introduced of creating digital autopsies through the use of a Computerized Tomography (CT) scanner. This allows the production of a three-dimensional image of the body enabling the pathologist to establish the cause of death without having to cut the body.

Caring for a person after death is the final act any practitioner can do for a person and it is vital that it is done in a respectful and sensitive manner both for the person who has died and for their family members.

The time following the death

Immediately after the death of someone the relatives are often busy with a number of practical tasks. Immediately there is the task of informing other relatives and friends of the death and making funeral arrangements. These may have been planned beforehand but often they have not. It can be distressing for families if they are not sure of the person's own wishes regarding their funeral. Some families do not discuss what they would like to happen after their death and are not sure whether the person would like to be buried or cremated. Some people think that by talking about death you somehow will it to happen. The one certain thing in life is that we will all die at some point. Talking about it will not bring it nearer but not doing so may cause distress to those we love who are not sure of our wishes.

Over to you

Answer these questions individually and then discuss with others:

● Would you like to be cremated or buried when you die? (or perhaps do something else like leave your body to medical science)

● Have you made a will?

● Would you like to donate any of your organs?

● Do you have a plan for your funeral?

● Have you chosen any specific music, readings, poetry etc.?

● Do those close to you know of your wishes?

It can be very comforting for relatives to know that they have fulfilled the wishes of the dead person regarding the funeral and it makes sorting out their estate so much more straightforward if there is a will.

In the first few weeks following a death there is generally limited time for the bereaved relatives to grieve as they are busy arranging the funeral, sorting out the person's personal effects and estate and there are often visits from other relatives and friends with offers of help and support. At this time the bereaved person may still be in a state of shock and the reality of the death may not have been fully realized.

As the weeks pass many relatives and friends return to their normal routines and are busy with their own lives. It is at this time that the people closest to the dead person can feel isolated and alone. This could be the spouse of the dead person, their children, parents or a close friend. Those that feel this isolation are generally the people who had most engagement with the person who has died, who saw them on a very regular basis, maybe daily or lived with them and who were very involved in their lives.

Sometimes it is people who were close to the person who died but were not known by other family members. This can be people from work or from areas of the dead person's life that they kept separate or hidden. Issues around this are covered in the chapter on unrecognized grief.

Some people feel awkward meeting people who are recently bereaved. They feel they do not know what to say so can avoid the person altogether.

Applied example

Robert and Jenny's daughter died suddenly just over three months ago. Since that time Roy and Jenny noticed that some of their friends and neighbours seem to be actively avoiding them. They saw one neighbour approaching them near some local shops. The neighbour glanced at them and hurriedly entered a nearby shop. Another acquaintance crossed over the road and hurried round a corner when she saw them. These reactions added to Robert and Jenny's feelings of isolation.

Others who do meet with the bereaved person may avoid mentioning that a death has happened. They may worry it will upset the person or feel they may get upset themselves. The death of someone close is upsetting and talking about it can result in tears being shed, but that can be helpful in demonstrating your care and concern for the person who has died and those grieving. It can also be a release of emotions and cathartic to express them with someone else present.

Applied example

Jane's mother had died and her aunt (her mother's sister) came to visit. Aunt Rosie talked about all sorts of things but never mentioned Jane's mother at all. It was as if her mother had never existed and Jane felt like shouting at her Aunt to say her mother's name so they could talk about her. In contrast, a neighbour came round and immediately told Jane how much she missed her mother and how she had really enjoyed her company. Both the neighbour and Jane were in tears as they talked about her mother, however, they both benefited from the opportunity to share their emotions and memories.

There can be for some a fear of crying and getting upset or seeing someone else in tears, particularly in a public setting. These emotions can be seen as unacceptable and to be prevented if at all possible. Others can be more open about expressing their emotions. Sometimes it is a cultural practice, either within a particular family or within a wider society that expression of these emotions are seen as either acceptable or to be suppressed.

People often feel they want to say something helpful when they meet a bereaved person. There are several platitudes that can be unhelpful for those grieving and can result in causing further distress rather than helping. Care workers and other practitioners can also make some of these comments without really thinking what they mean.

Below are some examples of *what not to say* to a bereaved person:

'It is all for the best' – although the person may have struggled with an illness over a long period of time it is unlikely that the death will be thought of by relatives as being the best thing that could happen to them.

'It will be alright' – when someone you care about has died, it is not all right.

' I know exactly how you feel' – you may have experienced the death of someone close to you and this may give you some insight into the experience of loss, but everyone

is different and we can never know exactly how another person feels

'Time is a great healer' – it is not the length of time after a death, but what the bereaved person does with that time that makes a difference in terms of working through the process of grief.

'You'll get over it' – this implies that you will forget about the person who has died and live your life as if they did not matter. If someone you are close to dies, then you do not want to get over it, you want their memories to remain with you.

A bereaved person will hopefully learn to successfully manage their lives without the person who has died and keep their memories of them incorporating them into their future life.

It can be a few weeks or a few months after the death that the bereaved person may seek support or help in wanting to talk to someone about their loss and how it is affecting them. Not everyone needs support in their grief from health, social care practitioners or voluntary organizations, and it is an area of debate as to what is the most effective type of support for the bereaved (Neimeyer, 2010). The death of someone we care about is a natural event we will all be likely to encounter at some time in our lives. How each person deals with this event can vary widely. It is estimated that about 10 per cent of people who experience a death seek help in managing their grief (Bonnano, 2009; Neimeyer, 2010). This help can be in a variety of forms. Some may ask for very practical help regarding dealing with the dead person's estate or finances. The focus of this book is on the emotional and psychological support that may be needed by the bereaved rather than practical or financial support.

Emotional and psychological support can be from a range of sources. Some health and social care settings, particularly hospices and community services such as Macmillan and Marie Curie offer support and counselling for the bereaved. Some acute hospitals have bereavement support services and there are several charities, who offer help and support to those grieving. Some charities focus on a particular section of the population in relation to bereavement. This can vary from certain types of death, for example, suicide or road traffic collisions, specific age ranges, for example, neonatal deaths or children and particular groups such as widows and widowers, students or those in certain occupations such as the armed forces or emergency services. The support offered by these services can be very varied and it is often difficult for the bereaved person to know what is available and identify what may be most appropriate to meet their needs. Details of the different types of support, counselling and psychotherapy services offered are explained in detail in the next chapter.

The support that the minority of the bereaved who seek help need, can be very varied. People seek support or counselling for a range of reasons. Some come because they do not understand what is happening to them and are worried that they are in some way abnormal or ill in what they are experiencing. Others may want to talk about the person who has died but feel they do not want to talk to family or others close to them. This may be because they do not want to upset others or that they feel awkward talking to people they know well about their thoughts and feelings. Talking to someone you do not know and having a formal professional relationship can be liberating for some people. It may facilitate them expressing their real feelings and share thoughts they would not like family members and close friends to know. An advantage some people like in seeing someone not known to them is that they do not have an ongoing relationship with the person and the time with them is limited to a set hour once a week or other fixed time frame. This creates clear boundaries for the bereaved person, which many find helpful. As counsellors and psychotherapists work to a code of conduct regarding confidentiality then this may give the bereaved person confidence to talk more openly to them. Some may have specific issues around the death or their lives without the person that they need help with.

It can occur particularly with people who have not experienced the death of someone close to them before. They are likely to be unsure as to what to expect and some of their experiences may seem odd to them. They may imagine they see or hear the dead person, even though they know they are dead. They may feel they have accepted the death and then find themselves crying uncontrollably or feeling so depressed they are unable to face other people or go to work. With these types of symptoms it is important to reassure the client that this sort of behaviour is normal. Often referring to certain theories and models of grief can help clients appreciate that what they are experiencing are recognized features of grief. It is usually not necessary to relate theories in detail but mentioning relevant details can be helpful.

Applied example

A client arrived looking anxious and related a range of experiences that had occurred since his partner, Sue, died three months ago.

He was walking down a busy street and was sure that he saw Sue in the crowd ahead, he recognized her hair colour and style. He rushed forward to reach out and touch her. He managed to stop himself as he reached the woman, realizing it was not her at all, it was just that her hair colour and style were similar. He spent the rest of the day feeling embarrassed imagining what would have happened if he had touched the woman and telling himself how ridiculous he had been.

On another day he was shopping and when he got home he realized he had bought some mackerel fillets which his partner loved and he doesn't like at all. He did not even realize he had bought them.

Some days he felt very calm and rationale, able to talk about Sue and relate stories about their life together, laughing at funny incidents. On other days the very thought of her brought tears to his eyes and he was not able to concentrate well at work. He found the unpredictability of his feelings very difficult to deal with. He would arrange to meet a friend but on the day be unable to go as he felt too upset or depressed. He could be sharp with friends, snapping at them and being irritable, which was most unlike his normal behaviour. He felt bad letting his friends down and was sure they must be fed up of him.

Some or all of these incidents related above can be commonly expressed by clients and be a cause of great concern to them. It is important not to minimize or discount these and to acknowledge the distress they may cause. It may be helpful to go through them individually. For example some responses may be:

Your mind will be consistently thinking about Sue even when you are not aware of it. Imagining you see or hear or even feel the dead person are quite common experiences and can be upsetting. You sound as if you gave yourself a hard time when this happened, how about trying to accept that this may happen and being pleased that you did not touch the woman.

You had lived with Sue for over 20 years and you have probably bought her certain foods she likes many times. It can be automatic to buy something she likes when you see it and it often takes a while for what has happened to register in our subconscious. There often seems to be a gap between the fact that we know intellectually that someone has died and the actions we carry out from habit or routine.

It is part of the grieving process that emotions and feelings fluctuate, sometimes quite dramatically within days and sometimes hours. There is no quick fix for grief. It is a process we all have to live through and the best thing is to be gentle and kind to yourself. Losing your partner of 20 years is a major event and it will take time to grieve. Be kind to yourself, do things when you feel like it and when you feel upset or depressed accept that is how you are today and do not push yourself or give yourself a hard time.

Grief can result in us behaving in ways we have not done before and can be quite alarming. Hopefully your friends will have some appreciation of that. Many people do not understand how grief can affect people and it may be helpful to talk to your friends explaining this. Some people think that within a month or so you should be back to your normal self and getting on with life. This is a major event that has happened to you and it does not get resolved in a matter of weeks. Your life will never be the same again and it will take time for you to adjust to living your life without Sue being a major part of it.

Explaining that the death of someone close is a major event and not one dealt with in a short time period can be very important in helping the client to realize the significance of what has happened to them.

Several clients may need to visit the practitioner on just one occasion as once they realize they are not 'going mad' as several clients describe their feelings and behaviours, they go away relieved that their experiences are normal and recognized features of grief.

Some may seek professional help as they feel their family is fed up with hearing their story or think they will upset others if they speak about the dead person. Coming for bereavement support can provide an opportunity for them to share their stories of the person who has died and they can derive comfort from this. It may also help them to formulate a biography around the person and their death, helping them to make sense of what has happened and the importance of that person in their lives.

For some, a current death may trigger past experiences of death which have not been resolved and so raise issues the person feels they need help to manage.

Applied example

Mary lived with her dog Jasper. One day a man came to the door with Jasper in his arms. The dog had run across the road in front of his car and the driver could not avoid hitting him. Sadly Jasper was dead. Mary was hysterical and could not be consoled. It was discovered that Mary's husband had died 10 years previously and at that time she had thrown herself into her work and other activities refusing to acknowledge his death. Jasper had been her husband's dog and Mary viewed him as a link with her husband. The death of the dog had brought thoughts of her husband back to her mind and she realized she needed to talk about his death even though it was so many years ago.

This demonstrates how the death of a pet can trigger responses from events in the past that people have tried to avoid. When a person starts to talk about a death it is not uncommon for them to link the current loss with previous ones that may not have been resolved. This can come as a surprise to the person as they may think they have dealt with the previous death, or that they have successfully avoided thoughts or feelings from that event. They can be amazed at the strength of their emotions once they start being open to their thoughts and feelings.

Working creatively

Some people find it difficult to sit and talk about their feelings and thoughts and to express themselves. They may also have complex relationships with their families and the person who died, which may affect their emotional responses.

Various items can be used to help people to talk about and express themselves. Some people find it easier to talk when they are holding something or using an item rather than sitting across from another person with nothing but an open space between them. It may be that a person is able to draw what they feel more effectively than they can describe it, this could involve shapes, colours or items. They may draw a whirlpool saying that is where they feel they are or black could indicate their negative feelings. Others may be alarmed at being asked to draw something, so sensitivity is needed in offering this as a technique

Stones are often used to help clients talk about themselves and their relationships with others. From a selection of stones the client is asked to pick one and describe why they have selected that particular one. What is it about the colour, shape, size, surface that helps them to describe themselves? This can also be done with buttons, shells and other items. In complex family systems, stones can be laid out with distances between them indicating how close people are to each other. The stone representing the client can be used to explain their own support network and how close they are to others. This can be useful for both the client in picturing where they fit in the family and also for the practitioner to help them understand the family dynamics.

Conclusion

Working with bereavement involves supporting people before, during and after a death. Communication is a key issue in all these circumstances and how the bereaved are treated at this time can have a tremendous impact on their response to the death and their experience of the grieving process. It is only a minority of people who need professional support or therapy as a result of grief. Many people manage their grief through existing support networks and use coping strategies they have developed to help them manage other traumas they have experienced in their life.

Key points

A good death can include a range of features, for many it involves being treated with dignity and respect, being in familiar surroundings, free from pain and other symptoms, and having the company of specific friends/family members.

The development of communication skills are vital for all practitioners working in this area.

Specific skills are required in supporting the patient and relatives pre-bereavement.

It is important to know the wishes of the dying person regarding funeral and other arrangements, so these can be fulfilled.

Sensitivity following a death is essential, being there and being silent can be sometimes what is required.

Don't use platitudes.

The majority of bereaved people do not need professional support or therapy.

Working creatively can be helpful and needs to be used sensitively.

Further Reading

Donnelly, E. and Neville, L. (2008) *Communication and Interpersonal Skills*. Exeter: Reflect Press.

McCabe, C. and Timmins, F. (2013) *Communication Skills for Nursing Practice*, 2nd edn. Basingstoke: Palgrave Macmillan.

NHS National End of Life Care Programme (2011) *Guidance for Staff Responsible for Care after Death*. Norwich: HMSO.

Payne, S., Seymour, J. and Ingleton, C. (2008) *Palliative Care Nursing: Principles and Evidence for Practice*, 2nd edn. Maidenhead: Open University Press.

3 Practical and Professional Issues in Supporting the Bereaved

Introduction

Support for a bereaved person can have many variables. It can take place in diverse settings, be carried out by a variety of practitioners working in health, social care and voluntary organizations, and occur over a wide range of time periods since the death occurred. Some support can be very formal and be for fixed time periods, others can be informal and for varying lengths of time dependent on specific circumstances and time available. It is important to recognize that the majority of people bereaved, some studies suggest up to 90 per cent, do not require interventions by voluntary or statutory services, but manage their grief through their own resilience and social support networks (Currier et al., 2008).

This chapter will consider a range of settings and circumstances where counselling and support take place. Issues covered include the definitions of what is involved in support, counselling and psychotherapy and the preferred features of the physical environment where this type of work may take place. This can include health and social care venues and the client's own home. Other issues covered include confidentiality, boundaries and the number of sessions that may be available to clients. Individual and group support will be discussed in terms of the different types of support bereaved people may find helpful.

Support, counselling and psychotherapy: the difference

When struggling with issues following a death, the bereaved person may want to seek out some help and support, but can be confused by services available. Many people are not clear when they see support, counselling and psychotherapy services offered exactly what each of them involves and which may be most appropriate for their needs.

Support

Support is usually the name given to a service provided by people with no recognized counselling qualifications. It consists of listening to the bereaved person, offering support in the form of being alongside them in their grief and helping them to express their thoughts and feelings. It is often provided through national or local voluntary agencies. Some of these agencies do have volunteers who have professional training in counselling and are members of a professional regulatory body and choose to give their time freely as a volunteer. Other volunteers will not have completed a recognized training course in counselling. They may have experienced a bereavement them-selves or some other trauma and several charities have devel-oped their own training courses for their volunteers specifically aimed at supporting those who come to them for help. Their role is mainly to listen to the bereaved person, to help them tell the story of their experience and discuss any issues they have. It may also involve assisting the client in clarifying their own thoughts and in formulating plans and actions for their future. There are voluntary organizations that support people experiencing a death in a wide range of circumstances and also specialist organizations. The specialist organizations often focus on particular aspects of the bereavement. This could be the age of the person who died, the type of death or the occupational group the person who died was a member of. There is a list at the end of this book of some of the general and specialist groups involved in supporting the bereaved.

Counselling

Counselling is a more formal arrangement between a person who has a qualification in counselling and the person coming for help who is referred to as the client. It is an interaction in a therapeutic setting, which can be a health or social care institution. It can focus on relationships, beliefs, feelings and behaviours and also how the death is causing problems or issues for the client. Counselling can use different approaches and generally the counsellor and client work together to look at new ways of approaching their issues and how these may be resolved or managed in a constructive way (Walker et al., 2007). There are a wide range of counselling courses and many counsellors have undergone training to diploma, bachelor's or master's degree level.

Psychotherapy

Psychotherapy is described as an extension of counselling involving exploring in more depth the issues and concerns of the client. Past experiences, which are affecting the current situation, may be analysed along with other issues that are relevant to their current issue. The aim is to raise awareness and insight for the client of their own processes and ways they manage their emotions in times of stress and trauma. They may have destructive or ineffective coping mechanisms and new ways are explored that are constructive and more effective. Psychotherapists have usually completed formal training to master's degree level (Walker et al., 2007).

Having described the three types of interventions above, there is often an overlap of all three in working with a client who has been bereaved. People offering support often use counselling skills and counsellors may explore issues in depth using psychotherapeutic techniques. Psychotherapists are likely to help clients to tell their story as well as explore in depth issues from the past or coping strategies. Counselling and psychotherapy can be described as being on a continuum with counselling at one end and psychotherapy at the other. Where the dividing line is between the two is often debated and the range of interventions made by the therapist, whether a counsellor or psychotherapist, can vary depending on the needs of the client.

Different approaches to counselling and psychotherapy

As well as the different types of help on offer in counselling and psychotherapy there are a range of approaches used by practitioners that are not always widely understood by those coming for help. Below are brief explanations of a few of the ones commonly used.

Humanistic/person centred

This approach was developed by Carl Rogers (1951) and is based on the relationship between the practitioner and the client. The client is viewed as a unique individual who is the expert on themselves and how they respond to situations in their lives. The client is helped to find, for themselves, what the best solutions are for the issues they have or what coping mechanisms will best help them through their current experience. The role of the practitioner is to come alongside the client and support and encourage them to step out into new experiences developing a positive concept of self and managing their own lives.

Cognitive behavioural therapy

This is based on the theory that our thinking affects how we behave. If we have negative and destructive thoughts then this will affect how we behave both towards ourselves and to others. The cognitive aspect involves identifying a person's thinking patterns and how they interpret the world. The role of the practitioner is to help the client restructure their thoughts into being less threatening and making positive statements to themselves with the desired outcome being to reduce fatalistic beliefs and encourage people to take control of their lives (Walker et al., 2007). An example may be that someone feels isolated after the death of someone close, thinking they have no other friends. This may lead to them becoming withdrawn and becoming more isolated. Working with the client could involve questioning these thoughts and encouraging them to develop a more positive response of seeing opportunities to mix with people. Often tasks are given to the client to engage in a conversation, which could be with a neighbour or someone at work. As the person realizes they can talk to others they will hopefully gain confidence and their negative thought patterns will be replaced with more positive ones.

The psychodynamic approach

This approach was developed by Freud (1949) and is founded on the theory that there are repressed memories from childhood that are not in the conscious memory, but determine how you behave and think today. These can result in a person using inappropriate or destructive defences in terms of their responses to traumatic situations in life. The aim of this type of therapy is to make the unconscious conscious and undo unsatisfactory defences, helping the client to experience the repressed feelings in a safe environment and express them as an adult in a more appropriate way (Gross, 2005). The practitioner may interpret what is said by the client in order to help them gain insight into the connection between their childhood experiences and current issues.

Integrative approach

An integrative approach is one which combines aspects of other approaches. It is built on the theory that individual approaches do not have all the answers as to why a person may act or think in a certain way. The aim is to integrate different approaches in order to form a new and different approach. Most integrative practitioners consider the relationship between the client and practitioner to be the most important aspect of the therapy (Gilbert and Orlans, 2011).

There are many styles of therapy even within the same approach. It could be argued that many practitioners are integrative to some extent in that they use techniques and knowledge from other approaches in their practice.

The therapeutic relationship

The most important aspect of any type of therapy, whether it is support, counselling or psychotherapy is the relationship between the bereaved person and the practitioner (Egan, 2013). It can take time for this relationship to develop and it is important for the client to feel comfortable with and have trust in the person there to help them. By using the core conditions identified by Rogers (2002) in Chapter 2 the practitioner can establish a baseline regarding the qualities of empathy, congruence and unconditional positive regard. Regardless of the setting or the professional background of the practitioner these qualities are paramount to facilitate a safe and secure environment in which the bereaved person feels able to talk freely and share their concerns and issues.

Over to You

Think of a person you trust, feel comfortable with and are happy to talk to about things that really concern you.

What is it that results in you trusting this person?

Is there anything specific they do or say to make you feel comfortable and safe?

The relationship formed in this setting is often referred to as a working alliance. This consists of the practitioner and the client working together to create an atmosphere of trust and openness where both are able to express themselves (Egan, 2013). It has been found in research studies that the best predictor of success in the helping process is the quality of the relationship between the client and the practitioner (Goleman, 1995; Eriksson and Nilsson, 2008). This factor comes above any techniques or choice of approach used. The development and maintenance of this quality relationship consists of several features. Effective practitioners work to build up a good rapport with the client, increasing trust and creating a climate in which clients can openly discuss and work with their issues. Good practitioners are perceived as caring and positive, have good listening skills and are non-defensive (Donnelly and Neville, 2008). As the practitioner trusts and cares for the client, then this can lead to the client trusting and caring for themselves more. This can result in the client developing a better relationship with themselves and of challenging themselves to make changes in their lives (Egan, 2013)

Counselling and psychotherapy regulation

During the first and second decades of the twenty-first century discussions have been ongoing between the government and counselling organizations regarding limiting the use of the titles counsellor and psychotherapist to those who have met certain standards in terms of training and who abide by a recognized code of practice and ethical standards. These discussions arose because these titles are not protected and people who have done very limited or even no training can use them to describe the service they offer. At the time of writing, in 2013, there is voluntary registration of these two professions and in the United Kingdom the two main registration bodies for counsellors and psychotherapists are The United Kingdom Council for Psychotherapy (UKCP) and the British Association of Counselling and Psychotherapy (BACP). These bodies provide a code of practice that practitioners work to and set standards regarding training, ethical issues and supervision. If a bereaved person decides to seek out this type of support then they are advised to check that the counsellor or psychotherapist is registered with either of these bodies, as this ensures a certain level of training and that standards of practice are in place. Both of these registering bodies have websites where people can search for a practitioner in their geographical area and obtain details about the person's level of training and the specialist areas in which they work.

Choosing the type of help

A question that may be asked by the bereaved is which of these three types of help is most appropriate for them? The answer can be any, or none. Studies have found that the vast majority of people who are bereaved do not require outside support or professional help but manage their grief from their own internal resources and through their family and social networks (Bonnano, 2009, Neimeyer, 2010).

Those who come because of their thoughts and feelings following the death may come for reassurance that what is happening to them is considered normal. This is commonly known as the normalization of grief reactions.

Applied example

Jane's Father had died. She had been very close to him. She was in her 30s, worked as a solicitor and led a very independent life. She was shocked at her response to her Father's death and found she was not in control of her emotions, which was not normal for her. Some days Jane felt fine and could concentrate on her work and talk about her Father, relating anecdotes of their time together. On other days even the thought of him would bring tears to her eyes and she struggled to focus on her work. She was normally a very sociable person but sometimes did not want to leave the house or even answer the phone. She thought she must be going mad and came to see a counsellor worried about her unpredictable emotions

The room

The venue where the support or counselling takes place can be very significant in terms of creating a welcoming, comfortable and safe environment. A major issue that can arise is that of finding and equipping an appropriate room for this purpose. Definitions of an appropriate room can vary but there are some key factors that need to be considered.

The furniture layout and decoration of the room can have a significant impact on how the meeting with the bereaved person progresses, determined by whether the client and practitioner feel comfortable and relaxed. A nicely furnished room gives out the message that the client is being cared for, that they are valued and it matters that they feel comfortable. A shabby, dark room setting can convey the opposite message.

A major factor is to ensure that the room is of an adequate size and preferably with natural light, not an interior room which is very dark and looks more like a store cupboard. In contrast a large cavernous hall is also unsuitable as it can be quite intimidating for a client in such a setting. Comfortable seats should be available, which are at the same height. This is so that both the client and practitioner are sitting at the same level. If one chair is higher it can give an air of dominance, particularly if used by the practitioner. Armchairs are preferable as office or upright chairs can be uncomfortable and not conducive to the client or practitioner feeling relaxed and comfortable. There are often just two chairs required in a counselling room but there may be another one or two if the room is used to talk with two or three people together. It is desirable that the decoration of the room is in muted pastel colours and plain, not bright and busy as this can be distracting for a client and result in them feeling apprehensive and uneasy. Soft lighting such as a table or floor lamp can add a restful pleasant atmosphere, whereas strip-lights or bright ceiling lights can be very harsh on the senses. Pictures on the walls, particularly of scenes of water, rocks or the countryside can also add to the calm atmosphere. A coffee table is useful for items such as tissues and there may be a dish of stones or other items that can be used in the session. A desk should not be in the room, particularly between the client and counsellor as this is not conducive to developing or maintaining a good rapport and could give the impression that the client is being interviewed.

Water may be provided for clients as a drink may be appreciated during the session. The room should not contain a telephone or if it does this should be disconnected during the session. Other disturbances should also be prevented by having a sign on the door saying the room is in use or some other system to make sure you will not be disturbed. It is not always possible to have a dedicated room solely used for this type of work. However, rooms can be adapted by rearranging a room used for another purpose. Moving furniture such as comfortable chairs or a low table into the room, or placing a table or floor lamp there can all have a big impact on changing the atmosphere

In health and social care settings there can be a range of issues that arise in relation to the physical environment available. For some bereaved people they may struggle to visit the same venue where their loved one died. This can be the case if bereavement support is provided in the hospital, hospice, residential care home or other venue which they associate with the person who has died. Others may be very happy to return to the place where their relative died finding it comforting to visit a familiar place and meet up with staff they already know. Below are examples of environments where bereavement support may be offered and issues that can arise.

Hospital

Issues that may arise for practitioners working in this environment will vary widely both between different hospitals and within hospital departments and units. Some hospitals have bereavement support services where practitioners offer support to the bereaved either on an individual basis or in a group. There may be specially prepared rooms, which are appropriately furnished and decorated for this purpose. Other practitioners may have to use rooms that are not specifically designed for this purpose so may need some adaptations, for example, a desk moving into a corner to enable the practitioner and client to sit without the desk between them. There may be the option for the bereaved person to receive support at another healthcare building, which they do not associate with the person who has died or one not related to healthcare at all. Some hospitals provide outreach services, which may be held in a local community centre where the bereaved can come to talk and receive support away from the hospital setting.

Hospice

Many hospices provide both individual and group support for the bereaved. The venue for this support is often the hospice and although some people may struggle to return to the place associated with their loss, others may find it comforting to return to the hospice and meet staff they know (Roberts and McGilloway, 2010). Many hospices have annual services and other events of remembrance, which are very well attended by family members and friends of those who have died there. Many bereaved people attend these events at hospices and welcome the opportunity to engage in a corporate act of remembrance. The format of these events and services can vary greatly. Some involve evening celebrations where lights or candles are lit to commemorate someone who has died and others can be a more formal religious service.

Community health or social care setting

These can be very varied and range from large council buildings to small community units, health or social centres. The rooms are likely to be multifunctional and may need some adaptations of moving in comfortable chairs and making them feel warm and comfortable with softer lighting if possible. Other issues that may be particularly pertinent to this setting are those of ensuring there are no interruptions and distractions. If the venue is used for other activities and groups then it may not be appreciated how easily sound travels or the need to ensure that the room is private and that other people do not interrupt the session.

Visiting clients in their own home

Visiting a bereaved person in their own home can have both advantages and disadvantages. The client will hopefully feel more relaxed in their own home and if they have mobility problems then this will help them to access a service they may not otherwise be able to take advantage of. However, there may be problems regarding ensuring a confidential space, free from interruptions in which to talk. It is good practice to establish at the start, what is expected, as some people will not be aware of the necessity of having a quiet, confidential space where you can both talk freely and not be interrupted. It is usual to meet with the person on their own in a room where there are no interruptions and no distractions such as a television switched on or people coming in and out. If two or more people are going to be seen together this needs to be agreed by all those involved. It is usually preferable to see people individually as if there are two or more family members together, this could inhibit what they may say in front of each other.

Confidentiality

A key principle in health and social care settings is that of confidentiality. It means making an undertaking to not discuss what the client talks about to anyone outside the setting without their permission and is a core feature in helping the client to feel safe and have trust in the practitioner. It is not possible to be absolute in agreeing confidentiality with a client as there are exceptions where the practitioner must inform others if certain things are disclosed. Some of the things practitioners must disclose to others are governed by law, some by their professional body's codes of conduct and some by the policies and procedures of their employers.

Examples of issues covered by law are the Children's Act (2004) and the Terrorism Act (2000). Under the Children's Act if a person discloses that a child is at risk of abuse or that abuse has happened then the practitioner has to report this to the appropriate authority. This could be the person responsible for safeguarding children in the practitioner's employing organization. If someone reveals a risk, or planned act, of terrorism then again the practitioner must report this and cannot keep this information confidential. Individual employers may have policies regarding what other information must be passed on to appropriate authorities in order that action can be taken. The issues covered by these could include adult abuse, potential harm to the client by themselves or others, or the risk of the client harming another person.

Many practitioners in health and social care will belong to a professional body that has a code of conduct containing standards on confidentiality. In the UK for counsellors and psychotherapists the BACP and UKCP are the professional bodies, nurses have the Nursing and Midwifery Council (NMC), and occupational therapists, physiotherapists and social workers have the Health and Care Professions Council (HCPC). All these professional bodies have a code of conduct that includes confidentiality and contain clauses that the practitioner must disclose information if you believe someone may be at risk of harm.

Over to you

Ruth is a client you are meeting for the third time. You feel you are developing a trusting relationship with her. Ruth says there is something she is concerned about and it affects her brother but before telling you, she wants you to promise you will not tell anyone else.

What would you say in response to Ruth?

It is important not to promise to keep something confidential before you know what it is that is going to be revealed. In response to Ruth in this situation it needs to be made clear that if she reveals that her brother is at risk of harm then you have to tell someone. You may say, 'If what you want to tell me involves your brother being harmed or at risk of harm then I must tell someone in order to protect him, however, when I know what it is we can then discuss what to do about the situation'.

Over to you: continued

Ruth then tells you that she has just discovered that her brother Tom, has not been taking his prescribed medication, which he needs for his heart condition since his father died as he does not see any point in living any more. He was already starting to be breathless and finding it a struggle to walk but he did not want anyone to know about this. Ruth is very worried and does not know what to do.

What discussion would you have with Ruth concerning this issue?

Talking with Ruth about possible options of who could help and support her brother may give Ruth choices of what she may do. Discussions concerning who her brother may be willing to speak to about his behaviour could be useful. This may be his general practitioner (GP) or another healthcare professional he may be in contact with. It needs to be stressed that it is not possible to know this information and take no action, as Ruth's brother was at risk of becoming very ill as a result of not taking his medication, and may have thoughts of suicide. In this scenario Ruth spoke to her brother and persuaded him to see his GP. The result was that he did start to take his medication again and through a referral by the GP became involved in a support group for the bereaved. Tom was reluctant initially to go along to this group but found it helped him to meet with others and share his experiences.

It is essential that there is clarity from the start between the practitioner and the client regarding the agreements around confidentiality. It needs to be explained fully to the client regarding the types of information that must be shared with others and hopefully the client will agree to these conditions. The word confidentiality can sometimes be used without either person being fully clear about what they actually mean by it, so it is important at the start of working with a client to agree on what you both understand by this and also the limits of confidentiality.

If the client refuses to give consent to share information the practitioner must still report their concerns to the appropriate person. An example of this is if the client expresses suicidal thoughts and explains plans they have made to end their own life. Even if the client does not agree to it, the practitioner must notify the client's doctor or other healthcare professional involved with the client of their concerns and what has been said.

Other exceptions regarding confidentiality could exist in certain settings such as hospitals, hospices and social care organizations where it may be appropriate and necessary to share certain items of information with other professionals. Clients should be made aware of what information may be shared and agree to this. It is important to establish and maintain the trust of a client so confidentiality should be closely adhered to. Breach of confidentiality should be considered very carefully before action is taken, however, the safety of the client is the main priority.

Practitioners who support clients need to have access to support for themselves and this is usually carried out through a process of supervision with a more experienced practitioner. The client should be informed of this, that issues may be discussed relating to them and that the supervisor is subject to the same code of confidentiality as the practitioner they are meeting with. If the practitioner thinks they need to break confidentiality with the client then they should initially contact their supervisor, if possible, to discuss this. Sometimes this is not feasible, for example, if someone is with you and expressing suicidal intentions, then you have to contact their doctor or mental health team but not all situations are as clear as this.

Boundaries

These are the limits that we place on our work and can involve a range of issues including the length of time the practitioner meets with the client to the range of topics covered (Gilbert and Orlans, 2011).

Formal counselling sessions usually last for 50 minutes, which is known as a counselling hour. Some counsellors do meet with clients for the full hour and at the start of counselling it is important to let the client know what the time constraints are regarding the length of sessions. The reason for the 50 minute counselling hour is related to the logistics of counselling. If counsellors are seeing two or three clients consecutively then the 10 minutes between clients allows time to arrange a further appointment for the client just seen, make brief notes if required and prepare for the arrival of the next client.

Over to you

Robert consistently arrived late for appointments and always blamed the buses or other people for his lateness. He then expected to meet with the practitioner for a full hour, as it was not his fault, as he saw it, that he was late. He also informed the practitioner that he is often late for work and other appointments as he struggles to manage his time.

How would you manage this situation?

Some clients arrive late and expect to be seen for the full 50 minutes. Boundaries need to be in place from the start letting the client know that even if they arrive late the session will end at the time arranged. Some people who come for support are not well disciplined in their own lives and it can help them if the practitioner is clear and consistent with boundaries. In the scenario above it may help Robert to be very clear about time boundaries and finishing on time even if he does arrive late. Talking about boundaries and helping him to take responsibility for his own time keeping instead of blaming others may also help him manage his time better in other areas of his life. It may be helpful to have discussions around how he can arrive on time, which could involve catching an earlier bus, allowing himself more time to travel or altering the time of the appointment if he comes straight from another commitment such as work.

Clients may want to stay over their allotted time and it is useful to remind clients as they are coming to the end of their time by saying things like 'We have 15 minutes left' and then 'we will need to finish in a couple of minutes' to make sure the client is aware of the time limitations and you can start rounding up the topic of discussion. Some clients will happily talk for well over an hour and be reluctant to stop. It can be difficult to get them to finish and some can bring up an important and significant issue right at the end of the session. This is sometimes known as a doorknob confession. Just as the client is about to go they will say something dramatic like 'I'm pregnant' or 'I am being made redundant'. The temptation is to feel you should ask them to stay and talk about the revelation they have just made. The appropriate response is to acknowledge the importance of the statement they have just made and say we will talk about it when we next meet. It can be argued that the fact that the client has waited until it is time to leave before telling you of this issue shows they do not want to talk about it at that visit, or that they are worried about it and only dare say it as they are leaving. The reasons for them saying it at the end of the session can be discussed when you meet them at the next appointment.

Another boundary that needs to be defined is the range of topics talked about in the sessions. When bereavement is the reason for the person attending for support, practitioners can at times be unsure whether to become involved in other issues that may be happening in the client's life and for which they want support. This can present a dilemma for the practitioner as to what issues are related to the bereavement and which are not. For any individual, events and circumstances in their lives are often interdependent. The physical, social, emotional, spiritual and psychological aspects of a person's life all affect each other. When someone close dies, this event is likely to impact on work, social life, relationships with others and spirituality as well as emotional and psychological health. In the process of working with a bereaved person in a therapeutic setting any or all of these issues may arise and need to be explored and managed. Issues around boundaries can also arise in relation to problems that were present prior to the bereavement. If a person has had long-term relationship problems with their partner over a number of years then this is not something that can be worked with and resolved through bereavement counselling. The bereavement may impact on the situation of the relationship and so can be talked about in that context but it would not be wise for the practitioner to embark upon relationship counselling when the focus should be the bereavement. Similarly if the bereaved person is finding it difficult to concentrate at work or having other problems at work related to their bereavement then it is appropriate to focus on this issue.

Number of sessions

Some organizations stipulate a maximum number of sessions that can be offered to clients. This commonly varies from four to eight sessions and some review the situation after a set number of sessions to decide whether more can be offered and if they are required. Other organizations have no limits at all on the number of sessions, so counselling could continue for a year or longer.

It is not possible to stipulate an ideal number of sessions that a person will require. Some may just meet with the practitioner on one occasion and that is all they need. This is often to be reassured that the emotions they are experiencing are normal, they will then leave comforted and able to manage their grief with the support of their social network and their own internal resources.

Others may have very complex responses to the bereavement and not have a social support network or internal resources of their own that can help them cope with their grief. These people may need prolonged support and help to build up their own internal resources and support network.

Another issue to consider is the time between sessions. Counselling generally takes place on a weekly basis so clients are seen at this time interval. Some practitioners may decide clients need longer to work through issues discussed, and so meet with clients after a two- or three-week time period. The time between sessions often alters as the counselling progresses. Initially weekly meetings may be arranged to give regular and frequent support. As the client develops skills and knowledge to help them manage their own emotions the frequency of meeting may be reduced to fortnightly or longer with regular reviews being conducted between the practitioner and client to ensure the support is at an appropriate level and frequency. The aim is to reach a point where the client feels able to manage their life without coming for support. It can be very rewarding to see a person who was, initially, in despair and seeing no purpose in life following the death of someone close, re-engaging with life, making plans and looking forward to their future.

Individual and group support

For some, meeting with a practitioner in a one-to-one situation can be a daunting and frightening prospect. The person may feel exposed and vulnerable in this setting, with all the focus of the practitioner on them alone. They may prefer to be in a group where they can listen to others and not feel so pressured to speak themselves. For others, being in a group can be frightening, with the risk of getting upset in the presence of people they do not know, and they may feel reluctant to talk with others around. Investigating the question as to whether individual or group support had better outcomes for clients, Currier, Neimeyer and Berman (2008) carried out an extensive review of 61 studies of grief counselling outcomes and found there were no reliable differences between group or individual counselling.

Having the option of both individual and group support can allow the clients to select for themselves which setting they feel would be most helpful to them personally.

Individual support

The advantage of individual support is that the individual receives the counsellor's full attention for the whole session.

They may feel they can be more open and honest in this confidential one-to-one environment, there may be things they would not like to share with a group of people or may feel inhibited if others are present. In this setting the relationship between the practitioner and the client is the most important aspect and requires skilled communication to both develop and maintain a trusting environment where the client feels safe to be open and honest about their issues.

Group support

Groups can vary greatly in terms of the numbers of people attending them, the period of time over which they operate and who leads them. Some groups are organized and led by practitioners who are trained in bereavement support and group facilitation. Others can be self-help groups organized and led by other bereaved people, where the group members support each other for mutual benefit. The size of the group is usually between seven and ten people. If the group is too large some members could feel inhibited to speak or not have the opportunity to express themselves in the time available. In a small group participants may feel exposed and it may be difficult to develop and maintain discussions. Groups for bereavement support are often fixed to meet for a set number of sessions, commonly eight or ten at weekly or fortnightly intervals. Other groups, for example, self-help groups established to provide mutual support, may be open ended and continue to meet as long as the members feel it is beneficial for them. Attending a group to talk about your responses to a death can be a daunting prospect. Concerns could involve anxiety regarding meeting people you do not know and the possibility of becoming upset or angry. These factors may prevent some people from accessing this type of support. For others, the prospect of meeting others who have experienced bereavement can be welcomed, and viewed as an opportunity to share experiences and both give and receive support. Some people may consider a group less threatening than meeting a practitioner individually, allowing them to listen to others and not feel pressured into talking themselves.

Applied example

A group for the bereaved was run for a period of eight weekly meetings. Six people attended from a variety of backgrounds and ages with a range of experiences in terms of bereavement. The group members were:

Sam, 23, his father died from cancer six months previously.

Mary, 60, her son had been killed in a road traffic collision four months previously.

Betty, 68, her husband died of a heart attack three months previously.

Sarah, 72 her husband died of cancer 2 years previously.

Kath, 60, her husband died of chronic lung disease one year previously.

Bill 48, his wife died of a cerebral haemorrhage eight months previously.

The people in this group had very different experiences of bereavement and were at very different stages of the grieving process. At the first group meeting ground rules were devised by the group members regarding the confidentiality of personal information disclosed in the group, listening and not judging each other and allowing others to be silent if they wished to be. During the group meetings members were able to talk about their experiences, share what was helpful and unhelpful for them in their situation, and offer support to each other.

Applied example

Sarah talked about how she had gone on holiday alone for the first time ever this year. Bill and Kath were very interested and asked details of what this was like as they wondered if they could do the same sometime in the future. Betty said she could not imagine ever doing that at the moment. Mary was waiting to attend the inquest into the collision where her son died and talked about her anxiety over this. Sam expressed how much he missed his father and that friends did not seem to understand why he was still getting upset, they expected him to be back to normal by now, as it was six months after his father's death.

Although the members of the group had very different experiences they were able to both give and receive support from each other. They found it helpful to hear of others experiences and for those further along the journey of grief like Sarah, hearing of her experience prompted others to consider whether they might be able to go away alone in the future. Sam was much younger than the others, however, he reported feeling very comfortable talking about his grief and that he considered he had more in common with the people in the group than some of his friends. Although all very different, members of this group developed good relationships with each other and several kept in touch afterwards meeting monthly for a coffee and to chat about how they were.

At the final group, members were asked for their evaluations of the meetings. All of them said they were apprehensive at first but were very pleased that they had come as they really appreciated talking and listening to others. They felt they had benefitted from meeting others even though their experiences were all so different.

This group demonstrated the value of coming together to share experiences, that they did need courage to attend initially but quickly realized that everyone had something to both share and to offer to others. The participants reported feeling less isolated, that they were not alone in their experiences and that it was okay to be upset, to talk about how they felt and that it was good to share these things with others.

This demonstrates that people from different generations and experiencing very different types of deaths have things they can share and can both support others and receive support themselves in a group setting.

Conclusion

There are a range of approaches that can be used to support bereaved people and a selection of settings where this can take place. What may be appropriate for one person may not be for another. Certain issues such as boundaries and confidentiality need to be clarified at the start of any support process and the availability of options available in terms of the setting and type of support offered needs to be clear.

Key points

Research shows that only a small minority of bereaved people require support from voluntary and statutory services to help them manage their grief.

The best predictor of success in the helping process is the quality of the relationship between the client and the practitioner, this comes above any approach or techniques used.

The titles counsellor and psychotherapist are not protected titles currently in the United Kingdom, however, there is voluntary registration with national regulating bodies.

Confidentiality is a key aspect of the helping relationship and is governed by laws, professional codes of conduct and policies and procedures of organizations providing the services.

Boundaries are vital in terms of timekeeping and of topics covered in the helping relationship.

Types of support required will differ depending on people's individual preferences and needs. Individual and group support both have advantages and provide for different needs.

Further Reading

Bonanno, G. (2009) *The Other Side of Sadness; What the New Science of Bereavement Tells us About Life after Loss.* New York: Basic Books.

Bor, R., Gill, S., Miller, R. and Evans A. (2009) *Counselling in Health Care Settings.* Basingstoke: Palgrave Macmillan.

Egan, G. (2013) *The Skilled Helper*, 10th edn. Belmont: Brooks/Cole Groups.

Gross, R. (2005) *Psychology: The Science of Mind and Behaviour*, 5th edn. London: Hodder and Stoughton.

4 Culture, Faith and Spirituality

Introduction

Culture, faith and spirituality can all affect how people respond to death, their grief reactions and how they mourn. These aspects can interact with each other or can be very separate. This chapter defines each of these issues and discusses the possible impacts of culture, faith and spirituality. Examples are given of particular faith and cultural practices. It is important to remember that within a particular culture, faith or spiritual view there are many variations, and there is a risk of stereotyping individuals belonging to certain cultures or faiths. It should never be assumed that a person from a particular group adheres to a fixed pattern of behaviours or rituals. It is useful to have some knowledge of different cultures and belief systems but also to be aware that the particular family you are working with may have their own interpretation of beliefs and practices to which they adhere.

Culture

Culture is defined as the beliefs, values, knowledge and practices shared by a particular group of people at a certain point in time. It can involve the way people dress, what they eat, their daily routines, activities and work practices. It can also involve specified roles for men and women in that group and even rules for what they are allowed to say and do. Culture can apply to people from a specific geographical area or from people who engage in a particular type of work. People who work in a certain industry, for example, banking, mining, civil service, healthcare may have beliefs, values and practices specific to that particular group.

Faith

Faith is a strong and unshakable belief in something, often without proof. It usually consists of a system of beliefs about something or someone. In religion it is often a belief in a higher being who has power and control over the world. In Christianity it is a trust in God, in his promises and actions. For other faiths it can be in higher beings, ancestors, animals or shrines. In some countries such as North Korea it can be the leader or past leader of the nation. It often involves various practices and rituals carried out in order to worship or pay homage to the higher being and sometimes to gain their approval and blessing.

Spirituality

Spirituality has been described as the very roots of our being; who we think we are, why we are here and what we should do with our lives (Wright, 2005). Even if a person does not believe in any higher being or power beyond themselves, then that is their spirituality, their spiritual belief system. Another definition is that spirituality is the search for meaning and purpose in life, which may or may not be related to a belief in God, or some higher power. This personal belief also shapes an individual's perspective on the world and is expressed in the way they live life (Johnston and Mayers, 2005). Clarke (2013) identifies certain themes that are present in spirituality. These include connection to parts of oneself, to other people, nature or the universe, and transcendence, that is, enabling a person to feel connected to something more powerful than themselves. This may be God, another higher power or a powerful spiritual energy, which is in the world. People may believe that this powerful connection can help them to cope with trauma and distress in their lives, giving them an inner spiritual strength and helping them find perspective and cope with their circumstances.

Following a death one or all of the above issues can impact on the responses made by those close to the deceased. The United Kingdom is a multicultural society and there are wide variations in practices among individuals from different cultures and also from those within the culture of our society. Some people will be strictly traditional and adhere to a clearly defined set of behaviours and rituals, others may be more liberal, adhering to some practices and not others. There may be some people who take practices from other cultures and adopt them as they feel they have meaning and relevance for them. Sometimes this can lead to conflict among family members who want practices to be carried out in a certain way. If the person who has died has left clear instructions of what they want to happen to their body and the format of their funeral service then this can help those left to feel that they have carried out the wishes of the deceased. If the person has not expressed whether they wanted to be buried or cremated, where they wanted their ashes spread or body buried, then this can cause distress as relatives try to decide what to do with the body or remains. For some cultures it is very clear as their practice is to always be buried or always be cremated and there are set rules for when, where and how this should be carried out.

Over to you

Questions to consider for those grieving:

- What are the cultural rituals for coping with death that are pertinent to this particular situation?
- What are the family's beliefs about what happens after death?
- What is considered a normal expression of grief for this family?
- Are there specific roles that certain members of the family are expected to fulfil in relation to the death?

If someone has left a cultural group or geographical area that was considered their homeland they may want their body returned to that area for burial or cremation. This may be very costly if a body needs to be transported to a country far away and may take time to arrange. For some people it is important to return the body to the person's native homeland and failure to be able to do this can cause great distress for family members.

Traditional funerals

Traditionally after someone has died in the United Kingdom the funeral directors visit the family and make arrangements for the funeral. If the family are connected to a faith group then a leader of that faith community is usually involved in planning the funeral service, choosing hymns or other music, readings and often will speak about the life of the deceased person at the funeral service.

There are traditional behaviours and practices that used to be common in the United Kingdom after a death that do not always occur now. These were to draw the curtains of the house where the person died and to stop the clocks. This was seen as a mark of respect for the person who had died. Immediate family and others close to the deceased would wear black for the funeral and often for several weeks afterwards. Men would wear a black tie and women would dress in dark colours or black. During the funeral, close relatives or friends may talk about the life of the person who died, or the faith leader may give a summary of the person's life. Some relatives who may like to do this may be too upset to be able to speak themselves so they may write out what they want to say and let another person read it for them. Traditionally, the funeral party leave from the house of the deceased to travel to the church or other place where the funeral will be held. There is a hearse containing the coffin and one or more official cars containing close family members of the deceased. Others attending the funeral follow the official cars in their own vehicles. When the funeral procession leaves the house it is common for one of the undertakers to walk in front of the hearse for a short distance. This may be just to the end of the street. Then the undertaker gets into the lead car and the procession continues to the church at a steady pace. People seeing a funeral procession or cortege as it is often called, may stand still as it passes and traditionally men wearing caps remove them as a sign of respect as the hearse passes by.

Secular society

Some people in a range of societies have no connection or

affiliation with a faith group or religion and may not want a funeral service in a church or other religious building. It is becoming more common for people to have non-religious services and ceremonies. These may be held at the crematorium if the person is being cremated and consist of friends and family speaking about the deceased, readings and music chosen by the person who died or their close family and friends and can be very varied. Following the burial or cremation a memorial service may be held celebrating the person's life. As it is a celebration there are sometimes instructions given to those attending asking them to wear a particular colour or colours and they may be asked to bring along items such as balloons or flags. There are an increasing number of people available to conduct secular funerals and families are encouraged to be involved in the planning and delivery of the service.

There follows below examples of some practices seen in different cultural and faith groups. It must be stressed that not everyone who is Irish, Hindu, Buddhist, Muslim or Jewish adheres to all these practices, they are guidelines of what may occur in these groups, and some individual families may adhere to just some of the following practices or carry out adapted versions of them.

Contemporary Irish society

Although some of the rituals that once surrounded death and burial have been lost in contemporary Irish society, more survives than is the norm in other areas of Western Europe. It is usually the intention of the close family to ensure that the person does not die alone. In Catholic families the death is usually accompanied by prayers and if the priest is not actually present at the time of death, he is likely to be called to anoint the body as soon as possible afterwards.

After death it is common to have the dead person laid out at home between the death and the funeral where friends and relatives can come and pay their respects. In Catholic homes it is usual for someone to be present by the corpse the whole time, and people will sit up all night to keep a vigil by the coffin. This is not usually the practice in Protestant homes.

It used to be the practice for men only to follow the coffin from the church to the cemetery with no women allowed. This is now changing but there are instances of women feeling that their own grieving has been hindered as a consequence of not seeing their loved one buried.

In Catholic communities a month to the day after a death there is an event called the 'month's mind'. This is a mass said for the repose of the dead person's soul. Anyone who could not get to the funeral will try to attend this service. Other masses are said on the anniversary of the death and every diocese has a 'Cemetery Sunday'; this is a day on which people visit the graves, tidy them and the Bishop or his representative comes to bless the cemetery.

Christian

There are many variations in the practices observed regarding death and dying within Christian communities and denominations throughout the world. Some are very formal and follow set traditions and others are more casual and unceremonious. In the Roman Catholic tradition, the rituals followed can be quite formal. When someone is dying the priest attends to give them the sacrament of the sick and pray with them. After death the person has someone with them until the funeral, keeping a vigil and praying for them. Other groups of Christians are often referred to as Protestants or Non-conformists. Protestants believe the bible is the sole source of revelation and Non-conformist is the term used to refer to Christians in denominations other than the Anglican Church. This term embraces a wide range of Christian groups including Methodists, Baptists, Pentecostals, house churches and independent evangelical churches. In Protestant traditions the leader of the church or other members may come and pray for the dying person and they may have Holy Communion by the bedside. In Non-conformist churches it may not be the church leader who does this but other members of the church congregation.

The funeral is usually held about a week after the death, there is no fixed time period for this to happen.

The Roman Catholic funeral service is traditionally very formal with set readings. Holy water is sprinkled during the service. The service consists of bible readings, prayers and Holy Communion.

At Protestant and particularly Non-conformist funerals the service can be much more informal and flexible in its structure. The service is likely to consist of hymns and other Christian songs, bible readings and prayers, which are said for the dead person and their family. Often relatives or friends will speak about the dead person giving a eulogy as a tribute to their life. As well as grieving for their loss, family and friends also celebrate the life of the person who has died.

Following the funeral service in the church, the body is taken to the cemetery for burial or for cremation at the crematorium, both are acceptable to Christians. At the graveside or at the crematorium final prayers are said committing the person to God.

There are no set time periods for mourning but Christians may wear dark colours or black to signify mourning at the funeral.

Following the funeral a memorial service may also be held to celebrate the life of the person who has died.

Buddhist

There is considerable variation between and within traditions and schools of Buddhism. Some funerals are very ritualistic whereas others are simple and solemn. Peace and serenity are hallmarks of a Buddhist funeral. Maintaining a peaceful and tranquil environment around the person who is dying is important. Upon death some traditions like the body to be left undisturbed for a minimum of four hours. During that time prayers are said and after this time the body can be laid out and moved.

Among Buddhists, family members wash the body after death, often using scented lotions and dress it in traditional clothes; this may be what is normally worn by the particular group. They are traditionally dressed in white which is the colour of mourning.

The first three days after death are considered to be particularly important as this is considered to be the time when the mind disengages from the body. If a postmortem is required it is requested for it to be delayed until three and a half days after the death (Rinpoche, 2013).

At a traditional funeral monks preside over the service delivering a sermon and performing Buddhist rituals. The family will wear white or cover their clothing with a traditional white cloth, along with a headband or armband. Mourners may also engage in other traditions. These include walking with a stick to symbolize their need for support, chanting or singing sutras (prayers), bringing offerings of flowers and fruit, burning incense and ringing gongs or bells. The Buddhist understanding of life is that death is not an end but a transition from one form to another. It is acceptable to show grief but the emphasis should be on understanding the transiency of life and performing good deeds on behalf of the dead person. The deceased may be buried or cremated but cremation is traditional.

Sri Lankan Buddhist mourners may return to work within 3 to 4 days and there are no restrictions on widows, although they may withdraw from social life for a time. With other groups of Buddhists such as those from Vietnam, there is a belief that a series of rituals following death will enable the spirit of the deceased to join the realms of the ancestors. The person who has died is especially honoured on the anniversary of their death and the lunar new year. Mourning lasts for 100 days during which time no one wears bright colours or flowers.

Hindu

Traditionally a Hindu will die at home, however, it is increasingly common for death to occur in a hospital setting. If possible a Hindu near to death will be brought home and have their family around them when they die. The family will keep a vigil until the person dies, singing hymns, praying and reading from Hindu scriptures (Hinduism Today, 2007). Traditionally a lamp is lit near the head of the person who is dying.

If the dying person is unconscious then at the point of death a family member will chant the mantra softly into the right ear, this is also carried out in the case of a sudden death such as a road traffic collision. The body is laid in the entrance to the home with the head facing south on a low bed or the ground, reflecting the return to Mother Earth, and a lamp is kept lit near the head. The body is washed by family members and close friends. Traditionally the body is washed in a mixture of milk, yogurt, ghee and honey, but may also be washed in purified water. While the body is being washed those carrying out this task recite mantras. Once the body is washed the hands are placed with palms together in a position of prayer and the big toes are tied together. The body is shrouded in a plain white sheet and if the person who has died is a married woman who died before her husband then she is dressed in red. If the person dies in hospital the family like to have the death certificate completed quickly so they take the body home. Organ donation is acceptable to most Hindus as there are no Hindu laws prohibiting this. In the home religious pictures are turned to the wall and in some traditions mirrors are covered.

In India the Hindu cremation is usually carried out on the same day as the death occurs. In Britain the first part of the Hindu funeral service takes place in the home due to the lack of time available in the crematorium. The body is placed in a simple open casket. The Pandit (priest) chants scriptures and the chief mourner, usually the eldest son performs rituals. Ash is applied to the forehead of a man and turmeric to the forehead of a woman. A garland of flowers is placed around the neck and holy basil is placed in the coffin.

The dead person is then taken to the crematorium where more prayers are said and the eldest son will press the button to send the coffin to be cremated. At the funeral service black is seen as inappropriate and white clothing is preferred. It is customary for men only to attend the cremation.

Returning home from the funeral all the relatives bathe and share in the cleaning of the house. A priest may visit and purify the house with incense. The day after the cremation the ashes are collected from the crematorium and traditionally in India these are immersed in the River Ganges. For Hindus living outside India it is becoming increasingly common for other rivers to become acceptable substitutes. There are companies that arrange for the ashes to be transported to India and submerged in the Ganges.

The period of mourning lasts for 10 to 16 days when the family is regarded as extremely impure and no other Hindu will receive food or drink from them. Furniture is removed from the room and the family live on simple food and without a radio or television. Between the 10th and the 12th day rituals are performed to enable the soul to form a new celestial body and join the ancestors. In the United Kingdom these rituals are carried out on the same day. Hindus believe that a delay in cremating the body could disturb the proper progress of the soul and prevent it from becoming an ancestor or being reborn. It can also upset the mourning procedures, which normally begin immediately after the funeral and so disturb the process meant to help the mourners adjust to the absence of the deceased. One year after the death the family observe a memorial event called 'sraddha', which pays homage to the deceased (Hinduism Today, 2007).

Humanist

Humanists believe that death is the end of a person's existence, that there is no soul or other supernatural component that survives after physical death. They view death as part of the natural order and a funeral as an opportunity for the living to celebrate the life of the person who has died.

There are humanist celebrants who will arrange and conduct funerals for those wanting this type of service and the person conducting the funeral will work with the family to plan the structure and content they would like for the service. A humanist funeral may include readings, music, poems and songs as well as tributes to the dead person. Tributes are an important aspect of a humanist funeral honouring and celebrating the life of the deceased.

Jewish

There is considerable variation among Jews regarding the observance of their traditional rituals in relation to death and grief. This can be dependent on their family origins, geographical location, degree of affiliation to their faith and personal beliefs and practices. The following details concern the traditional practices of orthodox Jews.

Death is seen by Jews as the natural and expected end of life: 'To everything there is a season: a time to be born and a time to die' (Ecclesiastes 3.2 King James Bible).

They have a tradition of expressing their grief through shared suffering and deal with death openly and directly (Herz-Brown, 1989).

Orthodox Jewish communities contain members of the Jewish burial society known as Chevrah Kadisha. This group arranges after death care and the funeral for the family of the person who has died. Jewish law dictates that the body should be ritually cleansed by someone of the same sex from the Jewish community. The Jewish view is that the body was once a person and should not be violated. Postmortems and any disfigurement of the corpse are forbidden unless required by law. If a postmortem is required, to discover the cause of death, it is sometimes possible to arrange for the body to be scanned through magnetic resonance imaging (MRI). This may be able to determine the cause of death, for example, in the case of coronary heart disease. This procedure is seen as more acceptable to many Orthodox Jews and some synagogues will pay for this to be carried out for members of their congregation. Orthodox Jews view the heart as the source of life and that it should not be removed, but most are agreeable to other organs being donated. The body should be allowed to decompose naturally and therefore should be buried and not cremated. Burial should take place as soon as possible after the death and in keeping with the separation of sexes at all Jewish services, men and women stand apart at the funeral service. A candle is lit for the benefit of the deceased, preferably in the room where the death took place.

Judaism has graduated periods of mourning, each with its own laws governing the expression of grief and the process of return to the normal affairs of society (Abeles and Samson, 2010).

Shiva, (means seven) is a period of one week from the funeral where the immediate family stay at home sitting on low chairs, do not wear leather shoes and receive visitors. They do not carry out everyday tasks and members of their community prepare all their meals. This gives the family the opportunity to reminisce and share amongt themselves and with visitors, memories of the person who has died. Communal prayers are conducted in the morning, afternoons and evenings.

At the end of *Shiva* normal daily activities are resumed but children mourning a parent do not attend any public events or entertainment for a 12-month period following the death.

Shloshim (meaning 30) lasts for 30 days from the burial, during which time the mourners return to work and resume their normal activities. In Israel it is the custom at the end of Shloshim to set the headstone on the grave.

Avelut is the name given to the year following a death, and at the completion of this time when all the annual anniversaries, Jewish festivals and significant times have been experienced by the mourners, there is a ceremony where a candle is lit. In the United Kingdom this is when the headstone is usually erected (Abeles and Samson 2010).

Muslim

There are different branches of Islam and not all will adhere to the same practices and rituals concerning death. There is an obligation in Islamic law for the sick to be visited, therefore there may be many visitors arriving at the home or hospital where the dying person is being cared for (Sarhill et al., 2001).

According to Islamic law, the body should be buried as soon as possible so arrangements for the funeral start immediately after the death. Family or other members of the community prepare the body immediately after death by washing and then wrapping the body in sheets of clean white cloth. This is carried out immediately as until the body is washed and prepared it is impure and those carrying out the ablutions are not able to say their prayers until they too have bathed. The strict rules that apply in life about the mingling of the sexes also apply in death. A woman may attend the funeral service but cannot look upon the face of the deceased if a male and a bereaved male cannot look at the face of a female who has died.

Muslims bury their dead immediately and funeral prayers are said at the mosque and the cemetery prior to burial in a deep grave facing Mecca. Traditionally women are not allowed to attend the burial at the cemetery. Islamic laws require friends and relatives to feed the mourners for three days and after this the family should return to normal life. During this three-day period, mourners receive visits and condolences and avoid wearing decorative clothing and jewellery. Widows observe an extended period of mourning lasting four months and ten days, during this time the widow is not to remarry, move from her home or wear decorative clothing or jewellery.

Great distress can be caused if a postmortem is required as this is seen as a desecration of the body. Therefore postmortems are only performed when the law requires this. For some Muslims organ donation is acceptable though there are considerable differences regarding this issue. Generally Muslims from Arab countries find organ donation acceptable but those from the Indian sub-continent do not (Sarhill et al., 2001).

Table 4.1 (page 78) gives information on practices from a range of faiths/beliefs. Several faiths have variations within them as seen with Buddhism, which has over 570 variations or schools, and Christianity, which has over 220 denominations. These subgroups within a faith system may have very diverse practices so the details in Table 4.1 should be used as a general guide with an awareness that there are likely to be wide variations of specific practices.

Contemporary practices

In the United Kingdom as in other countries, particularly in Europe and North America, there is an increasing popularity of natural burial sites and of environmentally friendly coffins. Natural burial sites are those which do not have traditional gravestones and where the burial of someone is usually marked by a tree or a shrub. Some sites do not allow any plaques or indication of who is buried there and trees or shrubs may be limited to those that are native to the country. The aim is to create a natural woodland where people can come and either walk or sit and remember the deceased without the area looking like a conventional cemetery. Natural burial sites can vary greatly in their size and regulation regarding types of trees and other structures allowed.

As well as traditional wooden coffins there are options to have coffins made of wicker, cardboard, papier-mâché or other natural substances such as sea grass. These are seen as being more easily biodegradable and with those made of cardboard or papier-mâché these can be individualized by the manufacturer regarding colours or patterns. Family members and friends sometimes decorate the outside of the coffin with messages or pictures prior to, or during the funeral service.

Matters to consider

A person may derive great comfort and security from their culture, belief system and spirituality following a death. Alternatively they may find these aspects hinder or complicate their grief. The belief in a life after death can be comforting to some as they may believe that the dead person has gone to a better place or that they will be reincarnated in a more favourable situation than when they were in this life. They may believe that they will meet the dead person again when they die and this can be reassuring. However, it could lead some people to want to hasten their own death in order to meet up again with the person they love. For those who do not believe in an afterlife, it can be particularly distressing to believe they will never see the person again. In western society, particularly in the Christian religion there may be additional distress if it is thought that the dead person has gone to hell and not to heaven. In Eastern religions such as Buddhism and Hinduism there is a belief that there is a progression of the soul following death. This involves the accumulation of good or bad karma (actions in this life that bring about consequences in the next), which determine a person's state in the next life with the ultimate goal of reaching Nirvana or enlightenment.

All deaths can be traumatic but some types can be seen as unacceptable or bring shame for certain people. Death by suicide is an example of this as in some cultures and faiths this

Table 4.1 Death rituals and requirements by belief/faith

Religion/belief system	Burial	Time between death and burial/cremation	Customs/rituals
Baha'i	Yes	24 hours	Buried within a 1 hour journey of the place of death. Prayers said by local Baha'i community
Buddhism (over 570 variations)	No	Within 1 week	The state of mind at the time of death is important in determining the state of rebirth after death. The body is usually kept at home until the funeral. Close family wear white, women wear a white flower.
			Simple service, Buddhist readings recited at the funeral. Believe that the spirit of the deceased will be reincarnated
Christian (over 220 denominations)	Yes	7 to 14 days	Funeral service in a church and may also be a wake or/and memorial service.
			Believe in resurrection of the human soul. Varied rituals for different denominations.
Hinduism	No	Within 24 hours	Want to die at home, lying on the floor, body returned to nature. If body left overnight may want lighted candle in the room. Eldest son lights funeral pyre or presses button at crematorium.
			Ashes scattered in the River Ganges in India. If not possible then at sea or in running water. Belief in reincarnation.

Humanist	Yes	7 to 14 days	Non-religious ceremonies tailored to individual needs. Believe in fulfilment in this life, do not believe in an afterlife.
Judaism	Yes	Within 24 hours	Body washed and prepared by fellow Jews. Jewish Burial Society arrange funeral. A 'watcher' stays with the body from death to burial. Son of the deceased lights a candle daily for 1 month and prays daily for 1 year. Non-Orthodox Jews may not adhere to all the above rituals.
			Orthodox Jews will not donate their hearts as this is seen as the centre of life.
Muslim	Yes	Within 24 hours	Body prepared for burial by relatives of the same sex as deceased. Prayers said around the body, often many relatives present and may be wailing. Body buried facing Mecca. Post mortem usually refused unless legally required.
			Most are reluctant to donate organs.
Sikh	No	Within 24 hours	Everyone must bathe as soon as they return home from the funeral, say a ritual prayer (Barsi) then have a meal.
			Emotions should be kept under control.
			Eldest son lights the funeral pyre or presses button in crematorium.
			Ashes scattered in sea or in running water.

is a cause of great shame. This can cause added trauma and pressure to those grieving this type of death.

Conclusion

The role of cultural heritage, religious beliefs and spirituality can be very varied among those bereaved by the death of a loved one. Supporting a family or individuals following a death involves showing respect for the family's culture and beliefs. In supporting them as they decide how to honour the death a number of issues need to be considered

Understanding different cultures' response to death can help healthcare professionals to recognize the grieving process in individuals, which may be very different to what they may expect in their own culture. It can also help them to provide appropriate support to different members of the family. Interfering with a group's customs or trying to force people to conform to certain practices may interfere with their progression through grief and could have long-term effects for the people concerned. An important aspect to remember is that people are individuals and that what may be helpful for one person may be detrimental to another and that within a culture, tradition or belief system there are many variations.

Key Points

Cultural faith and spiritual issues can all impact on how a bereaved person responds to a death.

There are many variations between and within different cultures and belief systems and it is important not to stereotype people regarding practices and rituals they may engage with.

Further Reading

Abeles, M., and Samson, J. (2010) *A Time to Mourn; Reflections on Jewish Bereavement. Practices.* Bereavement Care, 29(1), 19–22.
Clarke, J. (2013) *Spiritual Care in Everyday Nursing Practice.* Basingstoke: Palgrave Macmillan.

Sarhill, N., LeGrand, S., Islambouli, R., Davis, M. and Walsh, D. (2001) The Terminally Ill Muslim: Death and Dying from the Muslim Perspective. *American Journal of Hospice and Palliative Care*, 18(4), 251–5.

5 Differing Perspectives of Grief

Introduction

This chapter will cover a range of topics including how the age of the person who dies may affect those close to them and possible issues arising from the death of an adult child, parent or partner. Multiple bereavements and complex family relationships are covered with discussions around complicated grief and the medicalization of grief with reference to the latest version of the Diagnostic and Statistical Manual of Mental disorders (DSMV). Specific behaviours that can develop as a result of bereavement such as panic attacks, self-harm and obsessional disorders will be discussed along with the question of referral to specialist services to help with these disorders.

The impact of age

The death of an adult could include anyone from the age of 18 years upwards. If it is a young adult who has died there is often, as with a younger child, the loss of what could have been if the person had lived. The person who died could be at university, embarking on a career, recently married, have young children or be involved in some other event in their lives. Whatever age they are those close to them may, in years to come, wonder what that person would be doing now if they had lived. This can be particularly poignant if the person who died had friends the same age with which the family maintains contact. As the friends get married, have children or move on in their careers this can be a constant reminder of the loss of what might have been for their family member. It is commonly remarked that parents should not be in a position of burying their children. The natural order is seen as parents dying first and their children arranging their funerals, not the other way round (Handsley, 2001).

The term older people can refer to a range of ages. Often as people increase in age their definition of what they think of as an older adult alters, age can be a relative concept. Below is a comment from a nurse:

When I was in my early 20s and patients in their late 40s died, I used to think they had lived most of their life. Now I am 44 I think it is no age at all and that you are not old until you are in your 80s.

It may be thought that people are more accepting of a death if the person is over 80 years; that they have lived their life and that is a natural time for it to end.

However, the longer a person has been living and has been in relationships with others the more they may be missed.

Death of a parent

For most people the first death of someone close to them is the experience of a parent dying. This can be very significant and cause a range of issues for individuals. Sons and daughters have never known life without their parents as they have been around since their birth. This is obvious but many people do not realize the impact this can have, even on independent adults who have been living away from home for several years. People can vary greatly on how well they relate to their parents but the death can still have an unexpected impact for those who did not feel close to, or had a poor relationship with, a parent. If there had been conflict or unresolved issues then guilt and regret at not sorting out or resolving the conflict can become an issue for the bereaved. When both parents are dead the adult child can suddenly realize they are now an orphan. They may be married and parents themselves, but they have now got a new label attached to them. For some, this may not be an issue, but for others they may feel a sense of loss that surprises them. As they realize they are now the oldest generation of their family they may gain a sense of responsibility for their own family and for their position, as holder of their family name.

Death of a spouse or partner

There can be a wide range of responses following the death of a spouse or partner. If a couple have been married for 50 to 60 years and one partner dies then this can be a very traumatic loss. Being with someone for that length of time can make it even more difficult when they die than for someone who has only been married or with a partner for a short time. There is an increased likelihood of a recently widowed person dying before those who are married and of the same age (Elwart and Christakis, 2008). Longitudinal research studies have found that in the elderly, following the death of a spouse, the mortality of those widowed is between 30–90 per cent higher than married couples in the first three months and around 15 per cent in months that follow (Johnson et al., 2000). People left widowed after a long marriage or partnership may find they are living alone for the first time in their lives. They may have lived with their parents prior to their marriage and have never lived on their own. They may find this new experience very difficult to adapt to and it may result in them being fearful and losing confidence in themselves. Others may enjoy this new experience giving them the freedom to travel and try new activities they had not considered before.

A cause of grief not always acknowledged and recognized is that of the death of an ex-spouse although it has long been recognized that a divorce can cause severe grief responses for those involved in this situation (Hunt and Hunt, 1977; Rollin, 1992). In a study of people who had experienced the death of an ex-spouse, Scott (2000) found that over 75 per cent of people had a grief response and of these the response of nearly 30 per cent was severe or overwhelming. There were a number of factors identified as influencing this grief reaction. These were the length of time since the divorce, whether the surviving spouse had achieved an emotional detachment from their ex-spouse and the existence of role ambiguity at the funeral. Another factor was the lack of understanding from family and friends who often did not recognize the need to offer support. This could result in the surviving ex-spouse feeling insecure and confused by their conflicting emotions and the need for them to be reassured and supported at this time.

Multiple deaths

Some people have a number of deaths over a short period of time. This could be three or four deaths in a period of two years. It may be deaths of a range of people from different areas of their lives including family, work colleagues and friends or neighbours. An example could be the death of a parent followed by a miscarriage and the death of a close friend. There could be the death of someone not so close, like a neighbour or work colleague, which could affect the intensity of the grief already being experienced. It could even be the death, real or fiction, of a person in a television programme or of a celebrity that could result in an increased concentration of feelings associated with the real death of someone close. The death of a pet can also affect the grief being experienced so it is not always the multiple deaths of people close to the bereaved that result in the person experiencing multiple deaths.

Multiple deaths can also be experienced by people who belong to specific groups or have certain conditions. Leaver et al. (2008) found in their study of people with Human Immuno-Deficiency Virus (HIV) that as individuals experience the accumulative deaths of partners, friends, brothers and acquaintances this has a detrimental effect on both their psychological and physical health resulting in depression, increased stress and poor immunity leading to a faster progression of their own condition.

Celebrity death

Throughout history individuals with special accomplishments, characteristics and abilities have always been subjects of celebration. This has included royalty, religious leaders, politicians and athletes. In modern society this status has developed to include mass media celebrities such as singers and those seen on reality television programmes. Fans can form vicarious relationships with these celebrities and after their death these relationships can intensify (McCutcheon et al., 2004).

The end of what, for fans, is an important relationship can result in a profound sense of loss and result in strong feelings and expressions of grief. This was seen in the deaths of Princess Diana and Michael Jackson where thousands of people left flowers and gifts at their homes and burial sites (Radford and Bloch, 2012).

This trend prominently came into focus at the time of the death of Princess Diana in 1997 and it is since that time that fans have increasingly felt the need to express their grief in public (Radford and Bloch, 2012). This phenomenon consists of mass mourning by people who do not personally know the person who has died but as a celebrity they are widely known through their public role. Some people feel they do actually know the celebrity even though they have never met them. The relationship with the celebrity may have developed from a range of sources including, their role in a television series, films, reality shows or through media coverage. This public outpouring of grief can come as a surprise to the individual themselves as to how strongly they may feel emotions of sadness, crying and being upset. If the individual is in a group or crowd with other mourners then these responses can often be magnified as they join with each other in this corporate expression of grief. This is known as group polarization, where expressions in a group are heightened or more extreme in comparison to how a person may respond if they were alone (Gross, 2005). People may feel shocked at how they acted in a particular a situation and may need reassurance and an explanation of why they may have behaved as they did. A recognized feature of this type of grief is that, although fans exhibit very intense responses to the death, these expressions are short lived and those bereaved move through their grief much more quickly than if they had a face-to-face relationship with the person (Radford and Bloch, 2012).

Roadside memorials

Flowers, cards, soft toys and other mementos attached to lampposts or on the side of the road where a fatal collision has occurred are becoming increasingly common. These have been called spontaneous shrines (Santino, 2001) and appear very quickly, often a few hours after the death and may stay for several days or weeks. As well as appearing in connection with road traffic collisions, these are now being seen at the site of other sudden and traumatic deaths such as house fires, murder, floods and other disasters (MacConville, 2010). In some countries such as Greece these types of memorials have been in existence for many years marking a place of death and often contain a lamp or candle, which can be lit in remembrance of the person who died. The findings from studies asking people, who create these memorials, for their reasons for doing so have suggested that they have two main purposes. The first is to remember the person who died, and the site may be visited, to leave flowers or other items at regular intervals and particularly at the anniversary of the death, at Christmas or at other significant times. The second purpose suggested is that the presence of the memorial is a warning to other road users of the danger of that site, and to encourage safer driving in that area (MacConville, 2010). However, these memorials have attracted the criticism that they can actually cause collisions as drivers can be distracted by them and some organizations place a limit on how long mementos can be left at a site following a death, although practices concerning this vary greatly (Churchill and Tay, 2008).

A more recent type of memorial is that of ghost bikes. This practice started in the United States in 2003 where a bike painted white was locked to a street sign near to the site of a cyclist's death. This practice has now spread to the United Kingdom and several are placed by cycling groups who campaign for safer conditions for cyclists on the roads (MacConville, 2010).

Complex family relationships

An increasing number of people are members of families where there has been divorce or separation and there are step families where parents, grandparents and siblings meet infrequently. These family structures are often referred to as reconstituted families. In these situations one person can be a key contact in facilitating access to one section of the family network.

Applied example

Dave was divorced from Sarah and he saw their two children every fortnight at the weekend. When staying with Dave the children often visited Dave's sister and family and also his parents. Following Dave's sudden death the children did not have any future contact with Dave's parents or his sister's family.

This situation and variations on this can mean that children and others lose the relationships they had with one part of a family. This is not always the case and there may be an effort on both sides to develop and maintain ongoing relationships, but this needs to be actively pursued as it is unlikely that it will just happen. If the breakup of a relationship is acrimonious with anger, hurt and bitterness persisting then it may be that a family will want to cut off all contact once the key link to that section of the family has died. This can cause distress on both sides for the section of the family that has been cut off and also for those who had relationships with them. There is often no simple solution and mediation may be required to try and find a solution which is satisfactory to all involved.

Complicated grief

Grief is a natural process that occurs after someone close dies. The question of when, and if, this natural process becomes a mental illness requiring treatment is an issue that causes much debate. For some cultures and religions there are set rules and practices regarding mourning and it may be viewed that anyone deviating from these practices could be viewed as being ill. Other people could take the stance that what may to others seem an extreme response is acceptable. For example, a person could keep a dead person's room in their house exactly as it was when they died and maintain this for many years.

Applied example

Paul's wife died seven years ago and he kept everything in his house exactly as it was when she died. Ornaments were in the same position in all the rooms, her clothes were in the wardrobe, her toiletries in the bathroom and he kept all her possessions. When the carpet in the sitting room needed replacing, Paul could not bear the thought of taking it to the tip as his wife had walked on that carpet. He bought a new carpet for the room but not wanting to part with the old one, he buried it in the garden. It was because of this action that his GP referred Paul for counselling as he viewed this action to be abnormal and Paul in need of help. Paul had a job where he was consistent in his attendance and performance. He cared for himself well, eating a good diet, keeping himself and the house clean and tidy and independently managed his finances and other household tasks. He was in his late 30s and did not socialize very much outside work. He related that he lived his life in a routine he had created for himself and did not consider that he had problems that needed counselling. He knew he could change his lifestyle and become involved in other activities and relationships but he chose not to. He was functioning competently in both his home and work life and had made choices to live as he did. Although it may not be as other people may want to live, Paul was content with his lifestyle.

In the Applied example (Paul) the practitioner met with the client on three occasions discussing his lifestyle and the actions he had taken. It was clear that Paul was very aware of what he was doing and why, and that his actions may be viewed as being odd by other people. However, he was content in his routine and his lifestyle and did not want to change how he lived his life. The practitioner was respectful of Paul's decision to maintain his current lifestyle and they parted with the agreement that if in the future he felt a need to talk to someone then he could contact the service again.

There are a range of behaviours and activities in which bereaved people can engage. These may seem abnormal or in some way indicative of illness to others. Some people create shrines to the dead person or regularly talk to them and ask their advice. Others may save the dead person's possessions for years refusing to part with any of them or use them.

Applied example

Jim and Barbara's son died suddenly aged 24. That was 12 years ago and his car was still parked on their drive. Jim and Barbara had not used the car or done anything to it. It was rusting, the tyres were rotting and there was a hole in the roof, but still it sat there untouched by anyone.

After 14 years, Jim and Barbara decided that it was time for the car to go and they arranged for it to be taken away for scrap. The couple were unable to explain what it was that prompted their decision, they said it just seemed the right time to arrange for the car to go and were comfortable with their decision.

People involved in these situations may not know themselves why, but for some there seems to be a right time for them to change things, dispose of articles or move on in some other way.

The medicalization of grief

There are a range of views of grief in modern society. Rapley et al. (2011) assert that distress and misery resulting from life experiences, such as bereavement have been converted by mental health professionals into symptoms and disorders in order that they can be categorized as mental illnesses. It has been recognized that the definition of mental illness can vary, dependent on the educational, economic, social, political and religious features of both the individual and the society in which they live (Szasz, 1974). It is asserted by Parkes (1996) that because grief will be experienced at some time by most, if not all of us, this does not mean that it is always a natural process and cannot be viewed as an illness. These differing views can lead to conflict as some may view what others perceive as extreme or abnormal responses as acceptable and understandable.

The Diagnostic and Statistical Manual of Mental Disorders, fifth edition (DSMV; American Psychiatric Association, 2013) is the US manual that provides definitions of all recognized mental illnesses. It is a text that is used in many countries, including the United Kingdom, by medical practitioners to identify and diagnose mental health conditions. This latest version of the manual was published in 2013. In previous versions there was an exclusion clause around bereavement in relation to the diagnosis of a major depressive illness. This meant that for clinicians involved in diagnosing someone with a major depressive disorder, guidance was given to help them distinguish between depression as part of the normal grieving process following a death and that of a major depressive disorder. This clause has now been removed and is an issue that has raised much controversy (Wakefield, 2013).

It is recognized that some of the symptoms used to identify depression such as insomnia, lowered appetite, sadness and difficulty in concentrating can be present following a death (Clayton et al., 1968). These symptoms are also present in depression and according to DSMV if a person has more than five out of nine depressive symptoms for a period of more than two weeks then they are said to have a major depressive disorder. Opponents of the removal of the bereavement clause argue that people can be wrongly diagnosed as having major depression when in fact they are experiencing a normal grief reaction to the death of someone close to them (Wakefield, 2013). Those who support the removal of this clause are concerned that people with major depression could be missed, resulting in risks, for example to people who are suicidal, and that grieving people are not immune to major depression (Pies, 2013). This debate and differences in opinion of whether grief is an illness or a normal process are, according to Wakefield (2013), likely to continue.

Grief and time

It is common for bereaved people to ask how long their grief will last. We live in a society where we are accustomed to things happening quickly and many people want to know what they need to do in order to deal with their feelings of grief, resolve them quickly and move on with their lives. Many theorists are reluctant to specify set times and refer to grief symptoms being evident for long periods, but do not define what they mean by this (Stroebe et al., 1993). The time taken to achieve acceptance and adapt to a life without the person who died has been suggested by some to be an average of two to three years (Miller and McGown, 2008).

Grief is often referred to as a journey or a process that takes time involving adaptation to a new life in which the person who has died is absent (Wordon, 2010). Recovery has been defined as the restoration of stability enabling the person to undertake their everyday activities and move forward in their lives towards goals that have been redefined for their new life situation (Shapiro, 2008). They learn to live without that person, but there will still be times when they acutely feel the loss of that person even though it may be many years since they died. Grief will always be present for many people, but most learn to live with it and to manage their lives very successfully.

Applied example

Jane was attending the wedding of her niece Frances.

At the wedding service Jane thought about her mother and how much she would have enjoyed this event: seeing her grandchild marry and so many members of the family being together.

Jane's mother had died over 20 years ago before Frances was born so had never met her grandchild. This family occasion triggered an emotional response as Jane felt sad that her mother was not there to join in the celebrations.

It is not just the length of time but what you do with the time following a death according to Wordon (2010) that determines how you resolve your grief. He advocates a series of tasks (explained in Chapter 1) that the bereaved need to work thorough in order to progress through the grieving process.

It could be said that grief is never completed as there is always a loss present in someone's life if a person they cared about has died. It may be that the person manages their life very effectively and is involved in a range of activities and relationships, that they have accepted that the person has died and they move on with their lives. However, there may still be times when that person is missed and thoughts are present concerning them. Other people may not be consciously aware of the loss affecting them, they may view death as being part of life and move forward without reminiscing or having thoughts of what might have been if the person was still alive.

Adaptation to life following bereavement can depend greatly on a range of factors surrounding the death, what Miller and McGown (1997) refer to as external and internal mediators. External mediators involve aspects such as social support, whether the death was sudden or after a long illness, the socioeconomic status and religiosity of the bereaved and whether there are other concurrent crises. Internal mediators include the age and gender of the bereaved, personality type, existing health and level of dependency on others.

A personal attitude to the death can influence how a person progresses through their grief. Stephenson (1986) suggested that feelings of guilt and ambivalence are the most difficult emotions for siblings who are bereaved to deal with. If a person concentrates on the loss of the person they loved, how much they miss them and that their life is poorer without this person then they may develop a negative approach to life. However, if they are grateful for having known that person, have happy memories and concentrate on the joy and privilege they feel of having known and loved that person, then this can result in them having a much more positive attitude to their own future (Miller and McGown, 1997).

For some it is important to keep their grief. They want to commemorate anniversaries for the dead person and to keep their memories alive. An example of this happens nationally in the United Kingdom on 11th November each year (Armistice Day) as people gather at events remembering those who died nearly a century ago in World Wars I and II and in subsequent conflicts.

Others may not want to commemorate anniversaries or have events to remind them of their loved one. No one response is correct, it is what is right and feels comfortable for each individual, and what helps them to manage their loss and live their future lives.

Specific behaviours that may result from grief

Some people behave in certain ways following bereavement in an attempt to cope with their emotional responses. They may be aware of their behaviour or not realize that it is in response to the bereavement they have experienced.

Some people can develop harmful or destructive coping strategies, which can result in mental health illnesses and they may need specific help to deal with these. These can involve a range of disorders including self-harm, obsessional disorders and panic attacks, although these conditions are not always the result of a loss or bereavement.

Self-harm

Self-harm may be used by a bereaved person to help them release the pressure they feel inside themselves, which could be anger, fear, distress or another emotion (MacDonald, 2009).

Applied example

Amy was 14 years old. Her father had died suddenly when he choked one evening. He collapsed on the kitchen floor and although an ambulance was called and the paramedics tried to resuscitate him, he died. Amy and her mother were there at the time and after the event Amy became very quiet. It was two months later that Amy's mother discovered that Amy had been cutting her thighs with a razor blade to try and find release for the distress and anger she felt at her father's death. Her mother was extremely concerned and Amy was referred to a specialist adolescent service that worked with people who self-harmed. This service ran groups where adolescents talked about their self-harm and with the staff of this service worked on finding more constructive and positive ways of managing their feelings. Amy found this service very helpful and within a few weeks had stopped self-harming and found more constructive ways to express her feelings regarding the death of her father.

There are national and often local organizations that offer support and help for those who self-harm. There are also organizations that provide advice and support online.

Obsessional disorders

Obsessional disorders can involve people carrying out repeated actions often in a ritualized way. It is common for it to involve actions around hygiene. It can be the repeated washing of hands following a set routine or the cleaning of surfaces such as kitchen worktops. Other obsessions can involve security, repeatedly checking that the house doors and windows are secure or that the car is locked. These obsessions can seriously interfere with a person's life and may prevent them from holding a job or of managing their daily life. If they are constantly checking the house door is locked they may never get to the shops or to an appointment they need to attend. Cognitive behavioural therapy (CBT) works with the theory that it is the thoughts of a person that generate feelings and these result in certain actions. When the thoughts are negative then this can lead to an individual developing obsessive behaviour. By helping a person to change their thoughts, this can enable them to change their behaviour (Grisham and Williams, 2009).

Applied example

Tom thought that there were bacteria constantly on kitchen surfaces that would cause disease and death. As a result of these thoughts he cleaned the kitchen with bleach repeatedly to eradicate the bacteria. However, as soon as he had cleaned the surfaces he imagined more bacteria landing on the worktops and had to start all over again with more bleach. Once he had repeated the cleaning three times he felt some relief for a short while before he needed to start the cleaning again. He had a set method of cleaning the worktops and if he was interrupted by anyone during the process he had to start from the beginning again. He found he was spending several hours a day on this cleaning regime and did not have time to go to work or do other things as he could not go out and leave the kitchen for very long before he needed to clean it again.

Panic attacks

Anxiety is a normal human emotion felt in response to a stressful situation. This may be when someone feels they are in danger or if they are facing an important event such as an exam or driving test. Once the event is over or the situation changes the anxiety usually disappears. Panic attacks are different in that they seem to occur without an obvious cause and affect people in three ways: physiologically, psychologically and behaviourally (Tompkins, 2010).

Physiologically the person's heart rate increases rapidly and may appear to them to be very loud. They may feel dizzy, nauseous and unable to breathe easily as if they are choking. They may also have a crushing chest pain.

Psychologically, frightening thoughts may be present that the person is out of control of themselves, that something dreadful is about to happen, they are having a heart attack or a stroke and going to die.

Behaviourally the person may feel the need to run away, to escape from where they are. In order to try and avoid panic attacks they may refuse to go to certain places or to be alone.

Applied example

Sarah's father had died suddenly three weeks previously. She was very close to him, would speak to him every day on the phone and relied on him to help her with practical tasks. She did not know how she would manage without him. She started to experience panic attacks when she would suddenly become breathless, feel her heart pounding, be unable to move and think that she was going to die. These attacks lasted about three minutes but to Sarah they seemed to last for hours and she lived her life in fear of one happening again.

In helping a person with panic attacks it is useful to explain to them what is happening to them physiologically. The human body has a system known as the fight, flight or freeze response. In times of danger there is an increase of adrenaline production that speeds up the heart rate enabling the person to fight the danger, run away from it or stay very still and freeze, whichever is the most appropriate at the time. When a person feels anxious or under stress then the body can misinterpret this and thinking there is imminent danger increases adrenaline production, which leads to a rapid heart rate. The person becomes more anxious as they are aware of these changes in their body and so the spiral escalates into a state of panic.

There are a number of actions a person can take to help themselves during a panic attack. However, they may feel out of control and need someone with them initially to help and support them by talking through what they need to do (Tompkins, 2010).

Calming techniques involve slowing down breathing: count to four slowly as the person breathes in, get them to hold their breath for two seconds and then slowly breathe out to another count of four. This helps to calm the person and it is something they can do themselves when they feel a panic attack developing.

Self-talk can also be helpful in encouraging the client to tell themselves that they are safe, that nothing bad will happen, they can control it and it will pass.

Another technique is distraction. When the panic attack starts to develop the person concentrates on counting certain objects in the room or wherever they are or they picture a scene in their mind where they feel relaxed.

There are several self-help books and factsheets available and many local areas have support groups for people with anxiety related issues where they can meet with others and receive support.

Conclusion

There are many perspectives on grief and some people can be quite rigid in their views regarding what constitutes normal grief and what is abnormal. A widely held view is that an indicator of abnormal grief or that which needs specific professional help is when the person's grief is seriously affecting their ability to live and engage in daily activities of washing, dressing, eating, socializing, working, and so on, over a long period of time when they did engage in these activities before the death of their loved one.

Key points

Responses to death can vary greatly and can be affected by the age of the person who died, the relationship and whether the bereaved person has experienced other losses in recent times.

Complex family systems can result in bereaved people losing contact with part of their family.

There is considerable ongoing debate as to whether grief is a mental illness or a natural process.

There are specific behaviours that can result from a bereavement including panic attacks, self-harm and obsessional disorders

Further Reading

Gelder, M., Mayou, R. and Geddes, J. (2005) *Psychiatry*, 3rd edn. Oxford: Oxford University Press .

Radford, S. and Bloch, P. (2012) Grief, Commiseration and Consumption following the Death of a Celebrity. *Journal of Consumer Culture*, 12(2), 137–55.

Rapley, M., Moncrieff, J. and Dillon, J. (2011) *De-medicalising Misery*. Basingstoke: Palgrave Macmillan.

Scott, S. (2000) Grief Reactions to the Death of a Divorced Spouse Revisited. *Omega*, 41(3), 207–19.

6 Sudden and Traumatic Death

Introduction

It is recognized that the circumstances in which a death occurs can influence the way in which the bereaved respond, both in relation to the person who has died and towards others (Moos, 1995). This chapter will discuss what is meant by sudden and traumatic death and how these circumstances can affect the grieving process. A number of different types of death will be covered including: road traffic collisions; military and other conflicts; natural disasters; murders; and suicide. Other aspects of a death that may result in added distress are also covered. These include: where the body is not found; delays in arranging a funeral; inquests; police investigations; and court cases. The chapter will conclude with guidance on how to support people bereaved by sudden and traumatic deaths and particular health conditions that may be present.

Sudden and traumatic death

This phrase is defined as a death that was not expected nor the result of a long-term illness. It is often one that occurs as a result of a traumatic event and can happen to a person at any age. It can also be the result of an unexpected physical illness such as a myocardial infarction (MI), cerebra-vascular accident (CVA) or a sub-arachnoid haemorrhage that result in immediate death. Characteristics of a traumatic death are that there is no time for either the person who died or their relatives to prepare for the death, to say things they may have wanted to say, to say goodbye or to make plans for the funeral. Those experiencing the sudden death of someone close to them have been found to be more likely to experience prolonged psychological and physical responses than if the death had been expected (Lundin, 1987). There are general responses that may be present in all sudden and traumatic deaths and some very specific issues relating to certain types of death.

Common responses

A sudden death can result in a greater level of shock than with other deaths and the intensity of the grief experienced can take the bereaved person by surprise. They may be numb initially and not able to believe what has happened.

Applied example

Emily was a healthy 67 year old woman who had cycled into the village where she lived one afternoon as she often did. On return home she felt unwell. Emily went to lie down and collapsed with a cardiac arrest and died. One of her daughters who worked abroad was phoned and informed of her mother's death. Her response was 'My mother?' She could not believe that her mother who as far as she knew, was fit and well could suddenly have died. She thought she must be being informed of the death of someone else's mother.

Following the realization that the person has died, there is often a need for the bereaved to know the details, why they were in the place where it happened and as much detail as possible around the circumstances. Sometimes it can be confusing if the person was in a place where they were not expected to be at the time or doing something that was not usual for them.

Guilt can be an emotion that is particularly pertinent following a traumatic or sudden death. As the death was not expected there may be things a person wanted to say to the person who is now dead. They may have had an argument or said things they now regret when they last met with the person and there is no opportunity to rectify what they said or to say the things they really wanted to. This can be particularly traumatic for a person if they made a comment to the dead person wishing they were dead or had an argument with them parting without resolving their differences (Handsley, 2001).

A phrase often used by those grieving in this situation is *if only....*

Applied example

If only I'd said ...
If only I hadn't said ...
If only I'd done ...
If only I hadn't done ...
If only I had been here.
If only I'd seen her/him.

There can be a wide range of things that the bereaved can regret, this can add to their guilt and also result in them feeling they are to blame in some way for what has happened.

As the death is unexpected, those left may not know what the dead person wanted to happen in terms of a funeral, if they wanted to be buried or cremated. There could be differences between family members regarding this issue and if there is no will the person's possessions and property could be a source of conflict.

The people who may have witnessed the traumatic death or been involved in the event such as a road traffic collision can experience nightmares and intrusive images, which replay the whole event. This can be very distressing and lead to a condition known as Post-Traumatic Stress Disorder (PTSD). Details of this condition and how a person experiencing these symptoms can be supported are covered later in this chapter.

With a sudden death the need to blame someone can often be very strong. Part of establishing what has happened could involve finding out who can be blamed for the event. Sometimes the person who has died is referred to as innocent or to blame for their own death (Handsley, 2001). If the person has been killed by another person in what appears to be a random attack then they may be referred to as an innocent victim. However, if they die due to an overdose of illegal drugs or alcohol poisoning then they can be seen as to blame for their own death. The desire to blame someone can result in the bereaved wanting revenge and to have what they view as justice being done, with those they see as responsible being punished in some way. This can lead to people taking their own revenge on individuals or groups and keeping close contact with the police or others investigating the death.

Road traffic collision (RTC)

This phrase is now used in the United Kingdom for what used to be known as a road traffic accident (RTA). The name was changed as it is viewed that most, if not all collisions or crashes on the road are someone's responsibility and the word accident implies these events are unpredictable or a chance occurrence, which is not the case in the vast majority of cases (Davis and Pless, 2001). A death resulting from an RTC can be particularly traumatic to the bereaved if the driver responsible for the collision was under the influence of alcohol or drugs or should not have been driving, for example, being disqualified or did not have a licence. The bereaved family can feel very aggrieved that the person responsible was reckless and did not care for the lives of others by driving as they did. Following this type of death some families campaign for changes in the law to try and prevent similar collisions happening to others. Currently in the United Kingdom there is no roadside test for drivers thought to be under the influence of drugs as there is for those under the influence of alcohol. Following recent deaths resulting from collisions where the driver has taken drugs there is a campaign for roadside tests to be introduced as they are in some other European countries. Campaigning in this way can bring some comfort to grieving families as they feel they are doing something constructive to try and prevent other families having their experience.

RTCs are often reported in the media and this can be traumatic for relatives. There could be photographs of the collision site and vehicles involved, which may cause distress. If there is a particular section of road where several collisions have happened over a period of time then these can sometimes be mentioned in reports of a current collision. This could take families by surprise if an event affecting them several years ago is suddenly seen again on the news and can trigger their memories and emotions of the event.

> ## Applied example
>
> Emma was walking home with two friends from school in the afternoon. A car swerved onto the pavement hitting all three girls and killing Emma. It was discovered the driver who did not have a full driving licence, road tax or car insurance, was under the influence of drugs. The driver went to court and received a four-year sentence for causing death by dangerous driving and driving without a licence, tax or insurance and banned from driving for eight years. Emma's family were shocked to discover that there are no recognized police tests in the United Kingdom or statutory prison sentences for driving under the influence of drugs. They were very upset that this driver would be out of prison in a very short time whereas they had lost their daughter forever. This resulted in them campaigning for roadside tests being available for police to detect drug usage in drivers. They also campaigned for statutory sentences for this offence. The family derived some comfort from their campaign and they hope to affect changes, which will help other families and deter those using drugs from driving while under their influence.

There are investigations conducted following road traffic collisions and families may find it difficult to be asked questions about their dead relative and details of their movements on the day of the collision.

If other people were involved in the collision and survived, those close to the deceased may question why some people survived and others were killed. They may think that if only their relative had sat in a different seat in the car or bus, they would still be here. Other 'if only' thoughts could include if only the person was later or earlier travelling on the road that day, or if only they had taken an alternative route or had not chosen to make that trip. Post-Traumatic Stress Disorder is a condition that can occur as a result of being involved in a fatal collision and surviving (Taylor et al., 2001). Details of this condition are described later in this chapter.

Major disasters

This is where there are many people involved and can include a wide range of situations: collisions involving trains, aeroplanes and boats, natural disasters of earthquakes, floods, tsunami, hurricanes, volcano eruptions and other acts of nature.

These events often result in multiple casualties and deaths. It is recognized that a significant number of people affected by these disasters will suffer acute distress and will experience a range of mental health issues (Norris et al., 2002). Although the majority of people affected will recover without developing mental health disorders some will develop conditions such as depression, anxiety and complicated grief, which could arise several months or years after the event. The reactions of those who survive major disasters are reported as being shock, disbelief, anger, fear, difficulty in sleeping and eating and an inability to concentrate. This experience also shatters their assumptions that the world is a safe and benign place, or that tragedy happens to others and not to themselves (Asaro, 2001). Initially it may not be clear who has survived and who has not, so relatives can be waiting for news for many hours or days. Waiting and not knowing what has happened can result in people feeling as if they are in a vacuum, prolonging the impact of the disaster and increasing the likelihood of complicated grief (Kristensen et al., 2010). The person involved is not able to do anything to help the situation and as time progresses they may feel there is less and less hope of their relative being alive. It may be days following a large disaster that definite information is known and if the disaster is in a remote area or where access for rescuers is difficult then it can be even longer for news of casualties to become available.

The bereaved may in this situation want an answer to the question of why the person went to that place, particularly if it was known to be in an area with a high risk of a disaster occurring. They may feel angry at the person who has died for putting themselves in that risky situation and then feel guilty that they feel this anger.

Military

There have been deaths of military personnel in various conflicts in the world. If the death occurs in a geographical area that family members will not have visited or know much about it can be difficult for them to understand what has happened.

These deaths are often reported in the media and for some this can be a comfort. Others may find it distressing to see photographs and reports of the person they loved on the television or in newspapers. There is an issue for the military authorities concerning how quickly they can inform relatives of the death before they hear of the tragedy from another source. Messages can be sent quickly by mobile phone, email and other routes from the conflict area and also the media are quick to report a death through television and radio. It is important that the military services are able to inform relatives personally of a death and offer support before relatives hear the news from other sources. For example, the UK's Ministry of Defence policy aims to ensure that both military personnel and civilian family members are informed of the identity of a casualty as soon as possible (Cawkhill, 2009). The word 'casualty' in this context refers to a member of the armed forces who has been killed or is missing presumed dead. Although it is distressing to hear of a relative's death at any time it can be more traumatic if it is heard for the first time on the news or through a text message or email. There are often formal funerals conducted for military personnel that are organized by the armed services and may be held in a cathedral or other large church with coverage of the event by the media. Families may appreciate this recognition of what their relative has done for their country and that they are valued by their regiment or other military organization of which they were a part. Others may find this type of service impersonal and would have preferred a small, more informal family funeral. They may feel their relative's death has been taken over and managed by the military and that they have been marginalized or excluded from the event.

Conflicts

This can include a wide range of sudden deaths and can involve rival gangs, riots, demonstrations, individual conflicts and neighbour disputes. People in a group will often behave in a more extreme manner than the individuals would if they were acting alone (Gross, 2005). Individuals in a cohesive group with strong leadership will agree to extreme views, behaviours and actions that they would not consider acceptable as an individual. This can result in groups attacking people and causing injury or death as they follow the strong views expressed by the leadership of the group.

Some individuals can find themselves acting in a way they would not imagine as they become absorbed in a cause. There have been instances of neighbours being responsible for a person's death over an argument regarding boundaries or the height of a hedge. Emotions can be so strong that a person loses perspective and may act irrationally during an argument, not at the time being consciously aware of the consequences of their actions.

Murder/manslaughter

Homicide refers to the act of a human being killing another human being. Murder and manslaughter are the two offences that constitute homicide.

Murder is considered to be the most serious form of homicide and is where a person of sound mind unlawfully kills another person with an intent to kill or to cause grievous bodily harm (Crown Prosecution Service, 2012).

Manslaughter is said to have happened if any of the following three circumstances are present:

1. Killing a person with the intent for murder but where a partial defence applies: loss of control, diminished responsibility, survivor of a joint suicide pact
2. Where there is conduct that was grossly negligent leading to the risk of death and resulted in the death of a person.
3. Where there is conduct taking the form of an unlawful act involving danger that resulted in the death of a person.

The first circumstance is known as voluntary manslaughter as there is an intention to kill, the following two are known as involuntary manslaughter as there is not the intention to kill or cause grievous bodily harm (Crown Prosecution Service, 2012).

The distress and trauma experienced by relatives and those close to the victim following a homicide can be very extreme (Asaro, 2001). If it is not known why the person has been killed then this can increase the distress even more. There will be police investigations and often those close to the victim are questioned and can be suspected of being responsible. These events are usually reported in the media and this can cause added distress, particularly if assumptions are made regarding the person's lifestyle or behaviour. Other factors such as the level of violence used and the person being alone when attacked can affect the bereaved. The relatives may feel very disturbed at the violence the perpetrators used and imagine the fear and pain their relative may have suffered. In supporting those bereaved by murder Asaro (2001) recommends that it is important for practitioners to promote both safety and security in the physical environment where they meet with the bereaved person. This study also recommends that people bereaved in this way require the opportunity to discuss the murder, to explore questions of why it happened and to rebuild shattered assumptions about their world. They may also need to express feelings of anger or of feeling powerless.

As well as the types of death explained above there can also be other factors that affect the grieving process following a sudden or traumatic death.

Body missing

When the body of a person cannot be found, this can lead to both emotional and practical complications for relatives. It may be that the person is missing presumed dead and it may never be known conclusively that the person really has died.

Applied example

A man who was a very experienced sea canoeist was involved in running competitions off the coast of Indonesia. He knew the area well and one day did not return as expected from a trip out to sea. His wife raised the alarm and searches were conducted around the area. No trace was found of the man or his canoe. This area has many small islands and his wife was sure he would be on one of them having had a problem with his canoe. She could not believe he could be dead as he was so experienced and familiar with the area. After several months there was still no sign of the man and eventually he was presumed dead. It was not until he had been missing for over a year that his wife acknowledged that he may be dead.

In this situation the wife held onto the hope that her husband would one day reappear or be found on some remote island having survived their waiting to be rescued. Because there was no body it was not possible to have a place marked where the person was buried or cremated. The wife did decide to have a memorial service two years after her husband's disappearance and found that helped her to formally say goodbye and celebrate his life with friends and relatives.

In natural and other major disasters there are situations where all the bodies cannot be recovered and this can leave the bereaved wondering for years if their relative really was killed in that event and their hope may remain that the person is still alive. Where remains of those killed cannot be identified then these are often buried and a memorial is built at the site.

This has occurred in several venues including the massacres in wars and at sites of terrorist attacks (Pollack, 2003). It has been reported by survivors and family members as well as helping them restore the dignity of the bones of those who died it also enables them to have a place to visit to remember the dead and acknowledge what has happened (Pollack, 2003).

Delays

Following a traumatic death there may be delays in the relatives being able to arrange the funeral. This can happen for a number of reasons. If the police are involved in a suspicious death then a postmortem is often required to search for evidence and determine the exact cause of death. Relatives can find this distressing, however, this is often carried out as a legal requirement and even if relatives object the postmortem will still take place. The body may then be kept in the mortuary for a period of time meaning the funeral has to be delayed. This can cause added distress to family members who may feel they cannot start to adjust their lives to living without the deceased until the funeral is over and they have said a formal goodbye to their loved one (Riches and Dawson, 1998).

Other issues can arise if a court case is conducted following a death. Information about the deceased and their lifestyle may be revealed that was previously hidden or unknown by certain family members. This could involve illegal activity, lifestyle choices or hidden relationships, which may come as a shock to relatives and may add to their trauma. This information may also be published by the media, leading to notoriety rather than sympathy for the family and contributing to their further distress (Riches and Dawson, 1998).

Issues resulting from sudden and traumatic death

The goal of practitioners following a sudden death is to support and boost the resilience of the bereaved person and help them to use their existing social networks (Wade et al., 2012). However, some may develop specific issues that, although can be present with other types of death, are particularly significant in the case of sudden and traumatic death.

Shock

This can be a major issue for those bereaved in this way and may last for an extended period of time. It can last for days, weeks or even longer. The person may struggle to believe that the person really is dead (Asaro, 2001). The bereaved person may feel that there is an incongruity in how they are reacting. They may know in their head that the person is dead and they may even have seen the body of the dead person. However, they may in their heart believe that the person is still alive and expect them to arrive home at any moment. It is as if their mind and body are not connected and that the feelings in the body are lagging behind the head knowledge of the death. This can cause confusion for the bereaved person and may result in them becoming anxious that they are mentally ill. At this time they need support to be gentle with themselves. It often helps if they gently tell themselves that the person really is dead (Wordon, 2010). They may feel the person is still alive to them and talking about what they did together can help the bereaved person to create a story of the person, their relationship and help them to create memories that illustrate the importance of that person in their lives.

Anger and rage

Anger is a pure emotion, an energy that provides the necessary impetus and motivation to protect an individual across the physical, emotional, intellectual and spiritual aspects of their experience. It operates as an infrared sensor, delivering essential intelligence about the immediate environment. It signals a need to protect the self in a variety of life situations, particularly relationships and enables safe deep connections with those who may be very different in terms of personality or character. Anger sharpens thinking and articulation and deepens intimacy between individuals as unspoken wants, needs, opinions and ideas are shared (Parker-Hall, 2009).

The emotion of anger is of lifelong service in maintaining an individual's physical, emotional, intellectual and spiritual independence. It provides the impetus and motivation for taking necessary self-care action, and is a catalyst for confronting challenging situations, making new decisions and bringing about change. Anger is an integral part of the grieving and learning process, it is an antidote to depression and its expression is crucial to maintaining good physical health. Those who grieve are often surprised by the amount and strength of the anger they experience. It can be focused on a range of people including healthcare professionals, the dead person, relatives or themselves (Parker-Hall, 2009). It is important for the bereaved to express their anger appropriately and they may need help and support to do this. This can be in the form of suggested actions people can take or encouraging them to speak out their anger. Actions may include physical activity and can be very varied: playing a competitive game, going for a long walk, digging the garden or breaking old pottery in a safe environment can be very therapeutic for some. The person may not feel able to express their anger to relatives or friends but may feel freer to speak out to a counsellor or other practitioner.

Depression is often described as unexpressed anger turned inwards and that by expressing anger depression is avoided or resolved.

Applied example

Len's son Garry died of leukaemia at the age of 23. Len had a good relationship with Garry and they would regularly go for a drink together in the local pub. Several months after Garry's death Len revisited the pub with friends and enjoyed the social occasion. However, when he returned home he felt guilty and angry with himself that he had been out enjoying himself when his son was dead. In order to try to deal with his anger he stabbed his forearm with a screwdriver as a punishment for being out enjoying himself. Len repeated this practice several times. He sought counselling to try and find another way to deal with his anger. It took time for Len to begin talking about his feelings, but eventually he was able to express some of what he felt about his son's death. He also started to swim regularly in a local pool and was surprised that he found the exercise helped him process his thoughts and also to feel more relaxed.

Post-Traumatic Stress Disorder (PTSD)

This is defined as a response to a traumatic incident where a person has experienced, witnessed or been part of an event or events that involved actual or threatened death or serious injury to themselves or others (Newman, 2009).

There are a range of features that are characteristic of this condition; the person's response usually involves intense fear, helplessness, hopelessness or horror. Up to 70 per cent of people will experience some form of distress within a month of a traumatic event (Lee, 2012), some will feel 'fine' at first, and able to function normally in their daily lives, but repeated traumas can trigger feelings from previous events. Rescue workers and healthcare staff are not immune and some people experience PTSD symptoms following a serious illness or major surgery

Theories on the rationale for why this condition happens vary, however, it is thought by some to be based on three commonly held assumptions that people hold about the world and their place in it (Kirby et al., 2004).

1. *The world is meaningful and benevolent, a good place.* Although this belief is variable, most will feel comfortable

to live their daily life without the constant fear of an imminent disaster occurring.

2. *We view ourselves in a positive light.* Most people feel in control of their own lives and that they are generally able to cope with the untoward events and stresses they will meet in their lives

3. *It won't happen to me.* People know that others are involved in traumatic events and die as a result of collisions, conflicts, misadventure, attacks and so forth, but many do not believe it will happen to them. People may see reported in the media that a person has been attacked and killed walking in a remote area at night or driving too fast but they think it will not happen to them.

When a traumatic incident does happen to an individual or to someone they care about, this can shatter these assumptions of the world. As a result they can feel unsafe and threatened by their environment and those around them.

Specific symptoms of PTSD involve the following:

Hyper alert: The person has an over-reaction to situations. They may be startled by a noise outside, which others do not notice. It may be a car passing, but the person with PTSD is immediately alert and concerned that it is a threat to their safety. They may also be alarmed to be in closed or open spaces. They are likely to make sure they have an escape route if they are in a building, being concerned that they may be trapped. Alternatively they may not like to be in an open space as this makes them feel exposed and vulnerable to attack.

Fear and anxiety: The person will be over anxious with constant feelings of dread that something terrible is about to happen.

Avoidance: Certain situations will be avoided, this could be places or people and may also involve being withdrawn, avoiding talking about the event that traumatized them. Some people may try to block out their painful thoughts through the use of alcohol, drugs or other substances.

Memories: A common feature of PTSD is for people to have recurrent memories of the traumatic event. These usually take the form of reliving the event as if it is being played as a film in the person's head. The person relives the event in the present time as if it is happening now and experiences the same strong emotions as when it first happened. These memories can occur as dreams when asleep or when the person is awake breaking through their thoughts as flashbacks of the whole or part of the original event.

Anger: The person may look for revenge against those they perceive as being responsible for the trauma they experienced, or alternatively they may think they were to blame for what happened and feel they should be punished or punish themselves in some way.

Emotional numbness: In order to cope with the strong emotions they feel a person may become numb emotionally. This can result in being unable to show any emotions, either positive or negative. They will respond blankly to whatever is happening to them or those around them.

Survivor guilt: If other people died in the traumatic event an individual with PTSD may feel guilty that they have survived when others did not. If they managed to escape from a situation such as a train crash, they could feel guilty that they did not try to save others, even if they were not able to do anything more at the time.

Changed worldview: Their view of the world being a benevolent place and that they are able to cope with life can be shattered as they experienced a situation over which they had no control and were unsafe. This can leave them feeling vulnerable and may lead to them questioning why this happened to them or what they had done to deserve this trauma.

Self-image: While experiencing the original trauma they may have become upset or angry and done and said things they now regret. This can alter their own image of their self-worth and identity.

Depression: This involves feelings of negativity about the world, of others and of their own future. It may result in suicidal thoughts (Kirby et al., 2004).

Applied example

Dan was with the army in Afghanistan when an armoured car he was travelling in was blown up by an explosive device. His close friend was killed and he and other passengers were injured. Dan usually sat in the seat position where his friend who was killed sat on that day. He kept reliving the journey and asking himself why he sat where he did, feeling guilty that his friend died and he survived. He became withdrawn, not wanting to speak about what happened and becoming angry if anyone tried to encourage him to talk.

Supporting a person with PTSD

There are specialist services that provide support and treatment for people with PTSD. These can help the person deal with the trauma by helping them to recall and process the emotions and sensations felt during the original event, restore their sense of control and reduce the powerful hold the memory may have on their life. They can be reassured that the condition is likely to get better, for most people the symptoms disappear within 3 months of the event (Kirby et al., 2004). Allowing the opportunity to talk can help the symptoms to resolve. Acknowledging that this is a process that will take time can also be useful. This will help the person to gain some control over their experiences. Evidence suggests those able to talk about their experiences with empathic listeners are likely to recover more quickly. It is important to encourage the person to talk about the event in the past tense. If the person talks about the incident as if it is happening in the present then this can retraumatize them as they relive the experience. Talking about it happening in the past can store it as a memory of what did happen and not of what is happening now. If not resolved, the person may benefit from being referred for therapy with someone specializing in PTSD (Kalma et al., 2012).

There are several specialist techniques used in the treatment of PTSD (Kirby et al. 2004).

Trauma focussed cognitive behavioural therapy

This involves gradually exposing the client to thoughts, feelings and situations that remind them of the trauma and enabling them to think and behave differently when they occur. It also involves identifying thoughts that are distorted or irrational and replacing them with a more balanced view of the event.

Family therapy

PTSD often affects others in the family and by working together, communication between family members and relationship problems resulting from the effects of a person having PTSD can be improved.

Eye movement desensitization and reprocessing (EMDR)

This is a specialist technique involving elements of cognitive behavioural therapy. The client is taught to make rhythmical eye movements from left to right in a set sequence. It is thought to work by freeing the brain's information processing system, which is interrupted in times of severe stress.

Conclusion

Sudden and traumatic death can take many forms and the effects on an individual can be varied and diverse. Some may not have the strong reactions described above and others may have certain features more prominent than others. As with any other type of bereavement, the person should be responded to as a unique individual. It should not be assumed that the bereaved will respond in a certain way because of the type of death or level of trauma experienced.

Key points

It is recognized that the circumstances in which a death occurs can influence the way in which the bereaved respond, both in relation to the person who has died and towards others.

There are a range of events that can result in a traumatic and sudden death including murder, military and other conflicts, road traffic collisions and major disasters.

Shock, unbelief, anger and rage are common responses to a sudden death.

Certain features such as the body missing, delays in being able to have the funeral and media coverage can add to the trauma experienced by the bereaved.

Although up to 70 per cent of people will experience some form of distress within a month of a traumatic event, only a minority will develop PTSD.

Further Reading

Asaro, R. (2001) Working with Adult Homicide Survivors, Part II: Helping Family Members Cope with Murder. *Perspectives in Psychiatric Care*, 37(4), 115–25

Kalma, C., Cooper, C. and Robertson, M. (2012) *Psychiatry at a Glance*. Chichester: Wiley.

Kirby, S., Hart, D., Cross, D. and Mitchell, G. (2004) *Mental Health Nursing*. Basingstoke: Palgrave Macmillan

Riches, G. and Dawson, P. (1998) Spoiled Memories: Problems of Grief Resolution in Families Bereaved through Murder. *Mortality*, 3(2), 143–59.

7 Hard to Talk About Deaths

Introduction

This chapter covers the issues of deaths that many people find hard to talk about both for those bereaved and for those encountering them, either at work or at home.

The deaths covered in this chapter are those of a baby or child and death by suicide. Although these are very different from each other there can be reluctance for people to talk about these deaths with family and friends as well as with practitioners trying to support them at this time.

The first section discusses the issues surrounding the death of a baby or child. This can occur from before birth in terms of a miscarriage, to stillbirth and neonatal death, which is during the first 28 days of life. It then continues with the range of possible issues that can result from a termination of pregnancy and the death of a child.

A pertinent feature of the death of a child is that the death is occurring in the wrong order; it is frequently remarked that children should be arranging the funerals of their parents and not parents arranging this event for their children.

Miscarriage

A miscarriage is said to happen when there is the death of a baby from the date of a missed period up until 24 weeks of pregnancy (McDonald et al., 2011). After 24 weeks it is considered that the foetus is viable, that is, able to survive independently of the mother. After this period the death of a baby is considered a stillbirth or a neonatal death, covered later in this chapter. This is the current definition for the United Kingdom and other countries may consider the definition of a miscarriage differently by setting the time of viability of a foetus at either less or more than 24weeks gestation of the pregnancy.

A miscarriage is more common than many people realize. It occurs in approximately 10–20 per cent of pregnancies and results in 50,000 admissions to hospitals in the United Kingdom (McDonald et al., 2011). One in every hundred people who get pregnant has recurrent miscarriages. This is defined as having three or more miscarriages. The causes of a miscarriage can be varied and sometimes the reason is not able to be determined. Known causes include abnormality of the foetus, infections and blood disorders. There are certain issues that increase the chance of a miscarriage, these include: smoking, high alcohol intake and low or high body weight of the mother (McDonald et al., 2011).

Most people who have a miscarriage go on to have a successful pregnancy. The physical recovery from a miscarriage is usually uncomplicated and it can be regarded as a relatively minor condition from a physical perspective, however, the psychological effects vary widely (Evans, 2012). Some people may not be concerned about what has happened and assume that they will get pregnant again and will be successful in having a child. Others may be very anxious, worrying about whether this will happen again in a subsequent pregnancy. Some people may not tell others outside the immediate family that a miscarriage has occurred. As they often happen early in the pregnancy, before 12 weeks, then friends and family members may not be aware of the pregnancy. How the loss is seen by individuals will also vary greatly. Some may want to mark particular times that are significant to them in relation to the pregnancy. This may be when the baby was due to be born, what would have been the baby's first Christmas or other significant event. Other parents may not consider these issues at all (Evans, 2012).

It is often the mother who receives support following a miscarriage and the father can feel excluded or that their feelings are not important. Fathers can then feel guilty for wanting support or asking for help, feeling that they should be supporting the mother and not focusing on their own grief. A miscarriage is a loss to both parents, of their expectations of having a child and future plans they may have of when the baby was due (Kohner and Henley, 2001).

In supporting the mother it is important to allow her to talk about what is significant to her; not to respond with platitudes such as 'you can try again' but to acknowledge that this is a loss and that it is legitimate to mourn this loss. Some family members and friends may take the view that it wasn't a real baby as the miscarriage was very early in the pregnancy. The important issue is how the pregnancy and baby are viewed by the parents. With a late miscarriage, the parents may have had the opportunity to hold the baby and there may be photographs taken. Some parents find this very helpful but others may not, so it is a personal choice for parents regarding what is right for them at the time.

The first few weeks of a subsequent pregnancy can be a stressful time. Parents may worry that the same thing will happen again and be very anxious and conscious of the slightest indication that something may be wrong. Both parents and particularly the mother are likely to need support at this time. This can involve being available to listen to concerns and be supportive. It is never possible to guarantee that all will be well with a pregnancy, however, reassuring a couple that they are doing the right things in terms of eating a healthy diet, taking moderate exercise but also resting is likely to help them feel more relaxed (Kohner and Henley, 2001).

Stillbirth

A stillbirth occurs when a baby is born dead after 24 weeks gestation. The number of stillbirths in the United Kingdom was 5.2 per 1,000 live births in 2007 (McDonald et al., 2011). In approximately 40 per cent of stillbirths, the cause of the baby's death cannot be established. Ten percent of stillborn babies have some kind of abnormality and other possible causes are problems with the mother's health or problems with the placenta (McDonald et al., 2011). The effects of a stillbirth on the parents and also other close family members can be devastating.

The applied example provides a story of one family's experience and there are a range of responses that may occur.

Applied example

Dave and Nicky were expecting their third child. Nicky went into labour close to the due delivery date but during labour the rate of the baby's heartbeat dropped and it was decided to deliver the baby by an emergency caesarean section. Nicky was anaesthetised and taken to the operating theatre accompanied by Dave. The baby's heart beat stopped totally at this time. The medical staff informed Dave of this and needed to decide whether to go ahead with the caesarean section or whether to bring Nicky round from the anaesthetic to deliver the baby normally. Dave was very upset and asked the medical staff for advice. They advised that it would be better physically for Nicky to be brought round from the anaesthetic and to deliver the baby vaginally as that would be less of a risk to her physical health. Dave agreed to this, although he was very concerned at his wife having to go through labour to deliver a baby who would be dead. This is what happened and after the birth Nicky and Dave held the baby, a little girl, spending time with her and comforting each other. A photograph was taken of the child and foot and hand prints were made in plaster for them to keep.

Dave came for counselling two months after the birth of his baby to talk about his experience and how this was affecting him. He was worried about his decision at the time of delivery although his wife was supportive of this and assured him he was right to take the advice of the medical staff. He was finding it difficult to concentrate at work and to sleep at night. He also struggled to relax and found he easily got upset. He had returned to work four weeks after the birth and death of his child. Work colleagues, family and friends were all very supportive asking how his wife was coping and if they could help in any way. Dave felt it was not acknowledged that he had also experienced a loss and was feeling guilty for wanting support for himself as well as his wife.

Dave talked about his experiences in detail and how he was totally unprepared for this event. Their first and second children had been born after uneventful pregnancies and he had assumed the same would happen again. After three months his wife became pregnant again, which was what both he and his wife wanted. Dave explained that he could not relax and enjoy the prospect of having another child because he feared this child could also die. The pregnancy proceeded well for both mother and baby, but Dave remained anxious. Dave knew the chance of a second stillbirth was extremely unlikely, but he still worried about it happening. As the due date for this baby approached Dave talked about his worries and how he had not prepared anything for this child in terms of a nursery or equipment for fear of something going wrong. His wife went into labour a week before the due date and they had a healthy baby boy. Dave and his wife were thrilled at the new addition to the family. Following the birth, Dave attended counselling for one last time to celebrate his good news.

Some parents may feel anxious and guilty that they have done something that caused the stillbirth. This may be health related in terms of diet, smoking, drinking alcohol or physical activities such as sports. Sometimes parents want to find a reason for this happening, someone or something to blame. This could be the hospital, the midwife or doctor or an environmental factor such as living close to a certain industry. A feature of grief for some is to find a cause: they are unable or unwilling to accept that there is no known reason for the death. If no reason is found it can seem as if the event is unfinished, that there is no neat end to the story that provides a satisfactory conclusion as to why the death occurred (Walter, 1996). A significant aspect of experiencing a death through stillbirth is that the parents will not have heard the baby cry or make any other noise. They will have not known the personality of the child. This can add to the grief in that it is unknown what they sounded like or what their personality was.

Neonatal death

This happens when a baby dies after birth and before 28 days of life. The causes are varied. The most common reasons are low birth weight (under 2500g), prematurity, multiple births and congenital abnormalities. Predisposing factors include: the health of the mother, particularly the presence of chronic conditions, maternal age; there is a greater risk of this if the mother is under 20 and over 40 years; and the presence of infection (McDonald et al., 2011).

Many neonatal deaths take place in special care baby units where there may be specialist nurses or midwives to offer support to parents. Many parents will have very detailed memories of what happened in the hospital, who was involved in terms of staff and the sequence of events. This can be very comforting and reassuring for the parents or possibly distressing if the parents feel that the situation was not well handled or that there were issues and concerns around the care and treatment of the baby. Particular issues can arise concerning the continuance or withdrawal of treatment in a neonatal intensive care setting and parents can feel overwhelmed and unable to absorb information from health professionals at this time (Woodroffe, 2013).

In a multiple birth the death of one or more of the babies can result in mixed emotions for the parents. The parents may be so anxious about the health of the surviving baby or babies that they are unable to focus on grieving for the dead. This was the situation for parents who came for counselling following the death of one of their twins (see the Applied example).

Applied example

Phil and Grace had twins who were born at 29 weeks gestation. Both twins were very ill with breathing difficulties at birth and were cared for in the special care baby unit. One of the twins, Beth, died when she was 20 days old and the other twin, Amy, survived being discharged home after just over 3 months in the unit. Phil and Grace found that once Amy was at home and progressing well, that they were becoming pre-occupied with thoughts of Beth and were upset and tearful quite frequently. They could not understand what was happening as they were thrilled to have Amy at home with them, and came to counselling for help. As they related their story, Phil and Grace became aware that they had not really grieved for Beth at the time of her death. Life had been so busy, travelling daily to the hospital and caring for Amy that they had not given themselves the space to mourn for the loss of Beth. At the time of Beth's death they feared that Amy may also die and concentrated their efforts on caring for her. Now that Amy was progressing well, they could relax a little and as a result the feelings from the loss of Beth were surfacing. During the counselling sessions they talked about Beth and what the loss meant to them. They were able reflect on their experiences and gain some understanding of why these feelings were emerging now.

Following the death of a baby parents can welcome being given items relating to the baby to have as a keepsake. This can be a range of items, including the cord clamp, wrist bands and cot name card. Some parents want to keep the clothes the baby wore or the shawl they were wrapped in. A lock of hair may be kept and footprints, handprints and photographs may be taken.

Some hospitals have memory books or trees where the baby's name can be written as a permanent reminder and some have an annual church service in remembrance of babies who have died in the unit. Some parents find these remembrance items and events very helpful and others may not, so it is very important to be sensitive to the wishes of the parents and not assume that they will all want mementos. Sometimes parents do not want anything that reminds them of the death of their baby at the time it happens. However, if photographs, footprints or hand prints are taken these can be kept by the hospital in case the parents later decide they would like these items.

Termination

A decision to terminate a pregnancy is usually the choice of the mother and can be for a number of reasons. The pregnancy may be unwanted and a termination may be seen as the best way of dealing with this situation. The mother may have physical health problems and a pregnancy may put her life at risk. It could be that the baby is found to have a congenital condition, which is not compatible with life and therefore the mother decides to terminate the pregnancy. For some, a termination may be considered a way to solve a problem and it may be imagined that once carried out the mother will then resume her life as if nothing has happened.

However, an individual can have an emotional response to a termination that they did not expect. Certain aspects have been found to increase the psychological impact of a termination on the mother. These are: pressure from a male partner to have the termination, pre-existing low self-esteem, prior mental health problems and conflict with religious or cultural beliefs (Lipp, 2009). The person may feel after the event that they have destroyed a life and may regret that they will never know what that child would have been like. Some people many years after a termination will recall that the child, if they had lived would be starting school now, be 18 now or at some other significant stage of their life. Others may not think of the pregnancy as being a baby and not consider what would have happened if the child had lived.

It can be many years after a termination that a person has a reaction to this event.

Applied example

Gill was at a meeting with friends where the speaker was talking about families, suddenly she gasped and became very upset, crying and shaking. Her friends did not know what had happened and could not persuade her to talk about what had upset her. Later that evening Gill managed to tell her story. She had a termination when she was 17 years old (22 years previously). She had not thought about it for years but the speaker had talked about his child being born in the same month and year it had happened. Gill felt as if she had been hit by a huge wave of emotion. At first she did not realize what was happening but then realized the significance of the date being spoken about.

This demonstrates how people can be unaware of how a termination may affect them even decades after the event. Having chosen to have a termination a person may think they have no right to grieve, as it was their choice to end the pregnancy. In supporting a person who has had a termination it is essential to not judge the individual and support them in telling their story. It may have been a secretive event with no family members or friends knowing what happened and the person may still not want to tell others of this experience.

Death of a child

Parents assume that they will die before their children, that their children will be organizing and attending their funerals rather than them as parents doing these tasks for their children. This is a common theme expressed by adults and many express the desire for them to have died rather than their children who have not had the opportunity to live for very long (Keesee et al., 2008).

When a child or young person dies, as well as the loss of the individual there is also the loss of the anticipation of what may happen in the future. Many parents also feel that part of themselves has died along with the child (Malkinson and Bar-Tur, 2005). When a child is born there are often plans and thoughts of what the child may grow up to do and the planning of shared experiences. These may be specific activities like teaching the child to read, swim, play games, and the anticipation of spending holidays exploring places and having fun in parks. There may be plans about which school the child may attend and more long-term thoughts of what career the child may decide to follow, and their future life as an adult. This may even involve thoughts of potential grandchildren. It may be that those bereaved suddenly become aware of their thoughts for the future that they had not realized were there until the child dies. They may become aware they will never be grandparents (if the child was their only one) that they will never see them graduate from university or start their first job, get married, for example. With a very young child there are losses of experiences like taking the child to school on their first day in their new uniform and other such firsts. People often have friends and neighbours with children of similar ages and this can be difficult for a couple whose own child has died. There will be constant reminders of the other children engaging in activities that their child will never take part in. This can be difficult for friends and neighbours as well as for the parents. Neighbours and friends may feel awkward and even avoid the parents in order to avoid the possibility of upsetting them. It can appear to the bereaved parents that friends and neighbours don't want to associate with them anymore and can result in them feeling isolated and alienated from those around them. When a child dies and years pass there are likely to be thoughts about the dead child and what they would be doing if they were still alive. Examples are starting secondary school, sitting their exams, starting university or training for a career and starting their first job. There can be regret, bitterness and also anger that the child is taken away from them before they have had a chance to live their life.

The impact of grief on the family

There are some risk factors identified that can increase the risk of adverse grief reactions. These are: the death of a child through violence; the child is the only one in the family; and other losses occurring at the same time (Schut et al., 2001).

As with any individual, the way in which family members grieve can be very varied. Some may withdraw and not want to talk, whereas others may want to talk repeatedly about the child who has died. The bedroom of the child may be kept exactly as it was before they died with all the clothes, toys and other possessions remaining untouched. Another family may decide to dispose of everything connected to the child quite quickly after the death. One person may be very expressive in their grief openly crying and being upset while another may appear unemotional and involve themselves heavily in work or another activity. Everyone will have their own unique way of managing their responses to the death.

These differences can cause problems within families as some members do not realize the differences in expressions of grief. Assumptions may be made that those who are quiet or appear unemotional are not really grieving and do not miss the child. Those who are expressive or wanting to keep the child's room as it was before the death may be seen as not accepting that the child has died. When there are great differences between parents in how they express their grief there can be the irretrievable break down of their relationship resulting in divorce or separation. Siblings of the dead child can also be greatly affected by how the parents respond to the death

---

Applied example

Bethany was 10 years old when her sister Hannah aged 12 died in a road traffic collision as she was coming home from school. Bethany's mum was inconsolable and said there was no point in life now that Hannah was dead. Eight months after the death her mother was still refusing to go out and would sit for hours in Hannah's bedroom holding her soft toys and crying. She had not come to the school parents evening for Bethany and did not show any interest in her activities either in or out of school. Bethany felt her Mum did not care about her at all as she seemed totally focused on the death of Hannah and not interested in her at all.

A parent can be so distressed at the death of a child that they can become obsessional about their loss at the expense of caring for the child or children who are still living. In this situation a sibling who has survived may wish that they had died instead.

The death of a baby or child can have a dramatic impact on a family and it may be helpful for family members to be supported individually or as a group. The advantage of individual support is that the person can feel they are able to be more open about what they say and how they feel than if they were with other family members. An advantage of seeing family members together could be that they gain insight into how others are managing their grief. This could help them understand each other's responses and behaviours and enable them to support each other. It may be that the appropriate support is a mixture of individual and family meetings. This could provide the opportunity for individuals to express themselves more freely and also to work together as a family to support each other.

Suicide

Suicide is defined as the action of a person who kills themselves intentionally.

There are two perspectives concerning working with suicide in the area of bereavement. One is supporting a person who has had a bereavement through suicide and the other is of someone you may be supporting expressing that they have suicidal thoughts or ideations. Initially this chapter will cover the issue of someone having thoughts of suicide for themselves and then it will cover issues that may arise for a person who has experienced the death of someone close to them by suicide.

There is no single reason why people take their own lives. It is often as a result of a number of problems for the individual and they can see no other way to cope with their experiences. People may look for a cause, as if there is one factor that has led someone to take their own life. In reality, this act is usually a result of many factors.

Language can be an issue around suicide. Some people do not like the term *commit suicide* as it may sound as if the person has committed a crime. Suicide is not a crime in some countries but is in other countries and cultures. A term preferred by many referring to suicide is to *complete suicide* or to *kill themselves*.

Statistics

In 2011 there were a total of 6,045 suicides recorded in the United Kingdom. Of this number 4,552 were male and 1,493 were female. Over the past 10 years trends in these figures have remained stable in relation to the comparison of the figures for men and women. The age group with the highest suicide rate for males is 40 to 44 years and for females is 50 to 54 years (Samaritans, 2011).

It is acknowledged that the official statistics for suicide are lower than the actual figures, for a number of reasons. Some deaths are not recorded as suicide as there is some doubt whether there was the intention of the person to kill themselves. In this case the death may be classified as accidental or of undetermined intent (Samaritans, 2011).

Although a range of methods are used by people to complete suicide, it is more common for males to use violent and dramatic methods than females. It is more common for a male to shoot themselves, jump from a tall building, hang themselves or cut their throat. The more common methods for females are to take an overdose of tablets, or other drugs, drown in a bath or cut their wrists (Joiner, 2007).

Risk factors

There are a wide range of reasons why a person may kill themselves, however, there are some factors that increase the risk of suicide. These are: a recent loss; the breakdown of a close relationship; an actual or expected unhappy change in circumstances; painful and/or disabling physical illness; heavy use of, or dependency on alcohol/other drugs; a history of earlier suicide attempts or self-harming; a history of suicide in the family; or depression.

When a person is feeling low or distressed it may be that a seemingly minor event is the trigger for them attempting or succeeding to kill themselves.

Long term bereavement processes of older parents: the three phases of grief

There are several myths and assumptions around suicide that are incorrect (Samaritans, 2013).

- It is thought by some that anyone who attempts or completes suicide must have a mental illness. This is not the case. Although some people who kill themselves may have a mental illness, others do not.
- If a person talks about suicide they will not actually kill themselves. People who kill themselves have often told someone that they do not feel life is worth living or that they have no future. Some may have actually said they want to die. While it may be the case that some people who talk about suicide do not take any action it is very important that everyone who says they feel suicidal is treated seriously.
- A person, who has made a suicide attempt, is unlikely to make another. People who have attempted to kill themselves are significantly more likely to eventually die by suicide than the rest of the population.
- Talking about suicide is a bad idea as it may give someone the idea to try it. If someone mentions suicide it is important to explore their thoughts and discover if they have made any plans of what they may do to kill themselves. If someone feels suicidal they may not want to worry or frighten others and so do not talk about the way they feel. By asking directly about suicide you give them the opportunity to talk about this subject in relation to themselves.

Supporting a client with thoughts of suicide

If a person mentions thoughts of ending their lives in any way then it is essential to explore this issue with the person. As stated above, some people think that by exploring the issue there is an increased likelihood of the person formulating plans and taking action to kill themselves and that ignoring this issue is more appropriate. This is not the case and it is important to be proactive in this situation. The aim is to discover what the person means by the comment they have made and establish whether they have made any plans to kill themselves. If they have made plans and started to collect equipment to use it indicates that this is a serious situation in which the counsellor or healthcare professional needs to take action. This situation needs great sensitivity and asking about this subject could include a question as described in the applied example.

Applied example

Mavis had died three weeks ago and her husband Tom was feeling very lonely. They had been married for 63 years and Tom said he wanted to be with Mavis, he did not want to live any more. The counsellor asked him if he had thought about doing anything to end his life. Tom looked quite surprised, 'Oh no I would never *do* anything, I just don't know how I am going to cope without her.'

Sometimes a person will say they do not want to live any more without the person who has died, that they want to be with them, that they do not see any point in life without them, or other such similar statements. They may not intend to take any action and this communication may solely be made to express the strength of their feelings of grief. However, it may be that they do intend to join the person who died and be planning how they will do this. It is essential that the person working with the bereaved person explores what they mean by their remark and not make assumptions either that they do not plan to take any action or that they do.

If the person has made plans as to how they may kill themselves then it is the duty of the professional or other person working with the bereaved to take action. Making plans involves the client talking about a specific method they are planning to use, or equipment they are collecting. It can include a range of actions: storing up tablets and knowing how many they need to take to ensure they die; collecting equipment such as a rope and planning where to hang themselves and when; identifying a suitable knife; or identifying a suitable building from which to jump. If any plans are in place then this is a signal that the person is serious about killing themselves and action needs to be taken.

When working with the bereaved as a practitioner, at the start of the process certain ground rules need to be established. A very important one concerns the breaking of confidentiality. If the practitioner thinks that the person they are working with is at risk of harming themselves or another person then they will need to break confidentiality and inform someone of their concerns. The client or patient needs to be aware of this right from the start of the work. Who the practitioner informs of their concerns may vary depending on the circumstances. In a counselling situation the practitioner may talk to their supervisor and may have an arrangement to inform the General Practitioner of the person or a mental health team if they are involved in the care of the client. In a healthcare setting the manager of the practitioner will be informed and this may involve a mental health team or other medical personnel. It is important to inform the client of who is to be notified and preferably to obtain the permission of the client. However, if the client does not give permission it is still necessary to notify a designated person who can take action to protect them. This can be a very difficult situation for the practitioner working with the bereaved but it is vital that they do take action if they are concerned for the person's personal safety.

Supporting a person bereaved by suicide

Supporting a person in this situation can result in specific issues pertinent to this particular type of death, particularly in the area of social processes and the impact on the family (Groos and Shakespeare-Finch, 2013).

Inquests and delays

Following a death by suicide a postmortem and inquest are usually held. These are carried out to confirm the cause of death and to investigate the circumstances. It can be a distressing time for family members as it may delay the funeral and they may be upset at the prospect of a postmortem being performed. At the inquest details of the death may be given, which could cause further suffering. There may also be aspects of the person's lifestyle revealed that were not known about before. This could be a shock to family members, adding to their pain.

Stigma and shame

For some people there is a stigma surrounding the fact that a person has killed themselves to the extent that some do not admit to others the cause of death. They feel that it is not acceptable for someone to end their life in this way and family members or friends may think that this type of death reflects negatively on them in some way. It may be they think others view them as not providing enough support for the person who died or that in some way they were the cause of the death (Groos and Shakespeare-Finch, 2013).

> **Applied example**
>
> Paul ran his own business. He was struggling financially and this was having an adverse effect on relationships within his family. One day his wife, Helen arrived at the factory early in the morning and found Paul had killed himself by hanging. News quickly went round his family and relatives that Paul had died. There was an assumption that as Paul was under great stress at work, he must have had a heart attack. His wife did not deny these assumptions and this view was accepted to be the cause of death among his relatives and friends. At the time of Paul's death it seemed easier to Helen for her to accept these assumptions and she kept quiet about her husband dying through suicide. Two years after the death Helen went for counselling as she wanted people to know the real truth of how Paul died but was not sure how to tell people and was concerned about how they may respond.

People sometimes talk about suicide in hushed voices, as if it is something not to be spoken about openly or admitted to. This can add to the shame already felt by some about this type of death. There may be concern that dying in this way will affect others perceptions and memories of that person and that they will be viewed in a negative light. This was the case in the Applied example where Helen was very concerned about how family and friends would view her husband once they knew the truth about his death. Later she felt she did not want to keep this secret to herself any longer and wanted to be open and honest about Paul's death. She started by telling her sister who was very supportive and understanding of the situation and this gave her confidence to start telling others. Some were shocked and responded negatively while others were very supportive. Helen received strong support from her sister and some family members and friends and from her practitioner so although she did have some negative experiences she was glad she had decided to tell people the truth about Paul.

Guilt

This is a common feeling people express after someone they love has died through suicide. Many ask themselves and others if there was something they could have done to prevent the death.

Applied example

Emma was distraught that her best friend Kate had taken an overdose of tablets and killed herself. Emma and Kate had been at school together and had known each other for over 12 years. Emma was aware that Kate was struggling financially, and also in her work but had not realized how desperate she must have been. Emma kept going over in her head the conversations she had with Kate, Was there something she had missed? Did Kate say something that she did not pick up on? Was there something she could have done to prevent Kate from killing herself?

Those bereaved through suicide will often ruminate on their experiences with the person who died, analysing conversations and actions, looking for clues they may have missed that could have indicated what they were planning to do. Although some people talk to others about their plans or intention to kill themselves others do not talk to anyone. There are wide variations in what happens in the lead up to someone killing themselves. There is often a desire by those grieving to make sense of the death and find some sort of meaning in what has happened (Currier et al., 2006). It is important to realize that every adult has responsibility for their own lives and that no one has complete control over another person's actions. The exception is if the person is dependent for some reason such as illness or disability, in which case others may have responsibility for their wellbeing.

Sadness

Feelings of profound sadness are usually present in all types of grief, however a common feature present following a death through suicide is sadness over lost potential. There is the loss of hopes and *dreams* never realized, and all the things that could have been if the person had lived.

Anger

Those bereaved by suicide can express anger at the person who has died for leaving them. This can be for them escaping the difficult circumstances that may be present or for not thinking what effect their death will have on those left behind. This feeling is often associated with guilt as the bereaved can feel guilty that they feel angry with the dead person.

Relief

For some friends and family the weeks, months, and sometimes years, leading up to the death of a loved one through suicide have been a rollercoaster of emotion. In situations where repeated hospitalizations, crises of various types or other ongoing traumas have become part of life, it is normal to feel a sense of relief that the unpredictable nature of life has come to an end. These feelings are often linked with guilt or shame as the bereaved may feel it is wrong to be relieved that someone they care about is dead.

Applied example

Pam's partner John had bipolar disorder. Although he took regular medication he had times of deep despair and also of feeling unrealistically euphoric. He found his mood swings very distressing. He struggled to accept that this condition would be with him for life and decided to kill himself. He had talked about suicide to Pam but she had not realized he had actually planned what to do. He booked a hotel room for a day and took a very large overdose of tablets. He left a note saying he had done this in a hotel as he did not want Pam to find him at home. Pam was very upset at John's death but also expressed a feeling of relief that he was at peace now. She had been aware of his struggles and found it upsetting when he had his manic episodes feeling helpless to support him.

Conclusion

The death of a baby or child can have a dramatic impact on a family and it may be helpful for family members to be supported individually or as a group. There is a wide range of responses to this type of death and reactions of different family members can be very diverse.

Many of the issues resulting from bereavement by suicide are found in other types of bereavement. However, some of the issues have specific features such as shame and stigma that may not be present in other types of death.

If a bereaved person mentions anything related to ending their lives or the practitioner is at all concerned that this may be an issue then they need to explore this topic in a sensitive but clear manner.

Key points

The death of a baby can occur before during or after birth.

It is viewed as being in the wrong order for parents to have to bury their children as usually it is the other way round.

There is a great loss of what might have been if the baby or child had lived.

Family members can grieve in a range of very different ways and this can cause conflict and misunderstandings.

There are myths around suicide that if people talk about suicide or have made previous attempts they will not complete suicide. This is not the case.

Further Reading

Evans, R. (2012) Emotional Care for Women who Experience Miscarriage *Nursing Standard*, 26(42), 35–41.

Joiner, T. (2007) *Why People die by Suicide*. Cambridge, MA: Harvard University Press.

Kohner, N. and Henley A. (2001) *When a Baby Dies*. London: Routledge.

Lipp, A. (2009) Termination of Pregnancy: A Review of the Psychological Effects on Women. *Nursing Times*, 105(1), 26–9.

McDonald, S., Magill-Cuerden J. and Mayes M. (2011) *Mayes Midwifery: A Textbook for Midwives*, 14th edn. London : Baillière Tindall.

8 Unrecognized Grief

Introduction

In the case of most deaths there is an assumption that those with a close relationship to the dead person will grieve for their loss. Their right to grieve is validated both by those around them and the cultural norms of their society. The culture where individuals live or work contains norms and expectations that people adhere to in relation to their response to death. These govern areas of behaviour, affect and cognition. They also dictate what losses should be grieved over, how the grief is expressed and who is eligible to grieve. For some people in society this is not always the case and people with certain health or other conditions may not be seen as having the same rights to grieve as others. This chapter explores the concept of disenfranchised grief, how people with learning difficulties may express their grief and receive support and those who are bereaved of friends and relatives who have died with Human Immunodeficiency Virus (HIV) and Acquired Immune Deficiency Syndrome (AIDS) and also with dementia.

Disenfranchised grief

The concept of disenfranchised grief, is defined as the grief experienced by an individual but which is not openly acknowledged, socially validated or publicly observed. Kenneth Doka (2002) identified that some people who are bereaved feel unable to, or are not allowed to, express their grief, and developed the term 'disenfranchised grief' to describe this feature. He studied the impact of grief in what he described as non-traditional relationships. This included people who were having secret extramarital affairs, same sex relationships that people were not open about and other secret relationships of which friends or family members were not aware. Doka found that following a death in these types of relationships, while feelings of grief may be intense, resources for resolving or managing grief may be limited. Informal and formal support systems may not be able to be accessed as the relationship may have been secretive or unacknowledged by family and friends. Religious and cultural practices may also constrain the grieving process. If certain types of relationships such as those with people of the same sex are not acceptable to a certain cultural or religious group then the bereaved person may not feel able to inform people of their loss or to show any expression of their grief. Similarly if they were involved in a secret extramarital affair they may not want to admit even after a death that they were involved in a relationship with that person.

Disenfranchised grief can also be present in groups and societies where there are clear norms of who is seen as being eligible to grieve. These norms may also dictate what losses should be grieved over and how the grief is expressed. In accordance with these social norms, it may be viewed that close family members are seen as being the most eligible to grieve. This may exclude friends and colleagues who may have had close relationships with the deceased but feel their grief is not acknowledged.

The concept of disenfranchised grief being present in organizations was raised by Bento (1994). This concerns employees experiencing a death of someone close to them and being expected to function as usual at work after only a few days away to attend the funeral. There may be a self-imposed inhibition of expressions of grief by the employee in order to conform to the norms of the organization where they work. Bento states that any grief a person experiences can become disenfranchised if they are not allowed to express it in the place where they spend many hours of their week, which for many people is their workplace.

Doka (2002) identified three different categories of disenfranchised grief. The first is where the relationship between the bereaved person and the deceased is not recognized by society or by those close to the deceased. Folta and Deck (1976) identified that there is a commonly held assumption that closeness in relationships exists only between spouses and immediate family and that other relationships are often not recognized. This category of disenfranchised grief can be of two different types. One is where people are not expected to show expressions of grief as they are viewed as not being closely related to the dead person. They may be a neighbour or someone seen as an acquaintance rather than a relative or close friend. The other type is where a person or group are not informed of the death as those close to the deceased are not aware of the existence of these relationships.

Applied example

Jane had worked with Sue for several years and although she had moved away from the area over 20 years ago they kept in touch regularly and Jane visited Sue occasionally. Sue had a chronic respiratory illness and Jane made arrangements to visit her in September. In July, Jane wrote to Sue to confirm she was coming to visit and was looking forward to seeing her. In response to her letter, Jane received a phone call from Sue's sister whom she did not know and had never met. Sue had died in May. Jane was shocked and sad that she had not known of the death and had missed the opportunity of attending the funeral, which she would have liked to have done. Sue's sister was very apologetic and was unaware of Sue's relationship with Jane.

People often have many different social and other networks they are members of. This can include colleagues at work, members of a sporting club or interest group and social contacts in other types of organizations. The members of these groups may be very diverse and not be aware of each other's existence. When a person dies, a group may not be informed of the death as relatives do not know of their involvement in the dead person's life.

The second category of disenfranchised grief is where the loss itself is not recognized by the individual who is bereaved. The person may experience the death of a work colleague and may not realize that this has impacted on them emotionally. They may experience feelings and behaviours that are not usual for them such as being easily upset, unable to sleep, irritability and feeling depressed but may not connect these with the death of a colleague.

Applied example

Rachel worked in a care home and one evening her parents with whom she lived commented that she seemed very irritable and snappy and asked her why this was. Rachel became defensive and said she was fine, just tired. Later that evening, as she thought more about her day at work Rachel realized that she was upset because one of the residents she had known for a long time had died that morning. It was only when her parents commented on her behaviour that she realized the death had affected her more than she had thought.

The third category of disenfranchised grief is where the griever is excluded from activities of mourning and not given the opportunity to express their grief. This could include them being prevented from being involved in the planning of, or attendance at, the funeral service or other grieving rituals.

Applied example

Deborah and Frank had lived together for six years and did not have much contact with Frank's family. When Frank died suddenly of a heart attack, his sister and brother appeared and declared that they were arranging the funeral. They informed Deborah that as she and Frank were not married she had no rights to anything of his and his family would organize everything themselves. Deborah was very upset, she felt totally excluded from the arrangements around Frank's funeral. She would have liked to speak at his funeral but was told she could not do this as she was not part of the family.

This category also includes the situation where the bereaved prevent themselves from having any involvement in the funeral or other grieving rituals. This may be because they feel they are not a close family member or that they are not recognized as having a close relationship with the dead person.

Applied example

Bill and Terry had worked together for 15 years. When Terry started at the factory Bill had been a great support to him and they had always got on well. They did not socialize outside work but enjoyed working together very much. When Bill died, Terry wanted to attend his funeral. He would have liked to have said goodbye to Bill and pay his respects, but stopped himself from doing this. He did not know any members of Bill's family and thought they would not want him there – that he would be intruding on their grief.

Health and social care practitioners and disenfranchised grief

Those involved in health and social care can experience disenfranchised grief of which they may or may not be aware. Practitioners may view it as part of their role to deal with death and not realize that the experience of people dying has an impact on them. It may be that a particular death they are involved in triggers a memory for them of a family member or someone they know well and this can result in them having a strong emotional response. Practitioners can have varying attitudes to showing emotional responses when involved in patient or client deaths. Some believe it is never acceptable to show emotions in this situation and that members of staff needed to be composed and offer support to relatives and friends of the deceased in this situation. They may feel that acting in a composed manner demonstrates that they are competent and capable of doing their job, that showing emotions is indicative of a weakness, which could affect them in their future career.

Others consider it is important to show they are human, which means being open with their emotions in certain situations.

Applied example

Quote from an experienced nurse:

I know some people think it is wrong, but I have cried with relatives. I think it shows that we're human and that we care. I think sometimes we try and put a brave face on things and we come across as being quite heartless.

Supporting a person experiencing disenfranchised grief

As there are different categories of disenfranchised grief there are a range of types of support that may be appropriate.

Educating the client about what disenfranchised grief is can be very beneficial. It is not a commonly known term and an explanation of what it means may result in a person developing an awareness and understanding of what is happening to them. This can be a source of relief as they recognize their emotional responses as being due to the grieving process and this insight can be reassuring.

If the bereaved person has been excluded from any involvement in formal events such as a funeral they may want to create their own ritual or do something to mark the person's death that has significance for them. Examples of the types of activity people may find helpful are, saying a prayer, lighting a candle, placing a plant, ornament, statue or other item such as a bench in a special place or buying a specific item that reminds the bereaved person of their loved one. Some may want to have a special photograph framed or have a wall hanging or other item made to display in their home in memory of the person. The important thing is that whatever the person does should be meaningful and significant for them.

If the person feels that they are not eligible to grieve because they are not a close family member but a work colleague or a member of a social group the dead person was part of it is helpful to encourage the person to talk about their friend or colleague. As they describe their relationship and their involvement in each other's lives they will hopefully realize that they were important to each other and that now the person has died there is an experience of loss that is valid and important.

Learning disability

Learning difficulties can vary greatly in their severity, ranging from very mild where the person may have been able to attend a mainstream school, engage in work and live independently, to a person who may have both learning and physical difficulties meaning they are totally dependent on others for their physical and social care. When a person with learning difficulties is bereaved they may have additional issues – this can result in inadequate or inappropriate support.

An important issue to consider is the level of an individual's understanding of what has happened. It is very important to use clear language when talking to a person with learning difficulties about death. Using phrases such as the person has 'gone to sleep' or 'passed away' can lead to misunderstandings. Sometimes assumptions are made about the person's ability to understand what has happened. It has sometimes happened that a person with learning difficulties has not been told about the death but informed that the person has gone away or will not be coming to see them any more (Oswin, 1991). Reasons for not telling the person have been given as not wanting to cause distress to the person and a doubt regarding their ability to understand. However, doing this is likely to be very confusing and upsetting for the individual and deprives them of the opportunity to know the facts and to grieve.

Applied example

Peter was 24 and lived with his parents. His father died suddenly at work and healthcare professionals advised Sue, his mother, to not tell Peter immediately as he may not understand and this could affect his behaviour at home. Sue accepted this advice but found it very difficult not telling Peter and felt very isolated as Peter was their only child. After several days Sue did tell Peter what had happened and he did get upset. However, he was also very supportive of his mother and they were able to share their grief and comfort each other.

It may be that the person with learning difficulties is unable to express verbally how grief is affecting them and there may be other signs of changes that can be seen. These changes can be indicative of how grief can be manifested when the person does not have the vocabulary to express themselves.

Applied example

My husband died three years ago. At first my daughter Sarah, who
has learning difficulties and was then 34, would not talk about his
death. She would not attend the funeral but comes with me now
to the cemetery and we put flowers on his grave. She still won't
talk about him, but since his death she always follows me around
to make sure she knows where I am. She has put on weight for no
apparent reason and does not like doing some of the things she
used to really enjoy.

When a parent dies the person with learning difficulties may
worry that other family members may also leave them and they
then want to be with them at all times to make sure they are still
there. This can be a cause of great concern for the remaining
parent and they may feel they are not able to go out alone or
with others as their son or daughter will become distressed at
being left. This can be difficult to manage and the parent may
need support in this situation. If there are other people the son
or daughter know well and relate to then these relationships
can be encouraged and developed as it may be possible for
them to share in their care.

It is important to involve the person with learning difficulties in the planning of the funeral and for them to be given the
opportunity to attend. There are likely to be strangers coming
to the house following a death, this could be the funeral
director, members of the clergy or other person who will be
conducting the funeral and could also include health or social
care workers. This could be very upsetting for the person with
learning difficulties who may find it disturbing to have strangers around in what was normally a quiet house.

If a bereaved person attends a day centre or other organization regularly then it needs to be ensured that the staff are
aware of what has happened, so they can offer support and be
aware that any changes in behaviour could be due to the loss
experienced.

Sometimes a death can result in multiple losses being experienced. If the death is of a parent or the main carer the individual may be moved out of their own home where they have
lived for many years and placed in a residential care setting or

other type of home. This can be a great loss and lead to them feeling very frightened, isolated and insecure. When grieving, feelings of security and stability are very important so other changes that may be seen as minor at other times can take on a new significance. If a close friend or relative goes on holiday, or there are staff changes at a day centre these events can trigger feelings of loss and result in emotional and behavioural changes (Oswin, 1991).

If a person is unable to verbally express their grief it should not be assumed that they do not feel any. Relatives and staff can talk to the person about the death and express their sorrow, so the person has the opportunity to hear the spoken words and explanations. If they are able to express themselves then opportunities should be given for them to express their sadness and other emotions and for them to be helped to share with others what is happening to them. Groups can be a useful way of doing this and help people see that others have similar experiences.

Opportunities to remember the person who has died should be provided. If the person has to leave the family home because the main carer has died then explanations of what will happen to the home should be given and possessions should not be thrown out without involving the person with learning difficulties and giving them the opportunity to keep some things that are important to them. This may be an item not seen as having value: a well-worn cushion or a kitchen tool such as a spatula. These items may be very important for the individual to have and keep as it has significant memories and meaning for them. They may also like a framed photograph of the person who has died and to be helped to create a book of memories containing photographs, cards and mementoes. The person may need particular support at certain times of the year such as Christmas, Easter and other holidays (Oswin, 1991).

HIV and AIDS

HIV is a virus that is transmitted in body fluids, usually the blood. Its effect is to progressively destroy the body's immune system so it is unable to protect the body from infections.

This means people with HIV are susceptible to a wide range of infections and often need higher doses of antibiotics and other drugs. When the immune system has been destroyed to a certain level the person becomes susceptible to specific infections that people with a normal healthy immune system would not catch. If a person gets any of these infections they are then said to have developed AIDS and as the disease progresses the body is unable to fight infections even with large doses of antibiotics and other drugs. The person will eventually die of an infection that it is not possible to treat successfully (Mandal et al., 2004).

Applied example

Paul was homosexual and seven years ago he discovered that he had HIV. Over the past few years his admissions to hospital had become more frequent and prolonged as the disease progressed and it was becoming more difficult to treat his recurrent infections. Although he had been immunized against tuberculosis (TB) as a child, his immune system was so damaged that he lost his immunity and developed this condition. Despite being given large doses of anti-TB drugs Paul died. He was just 36 years old.

Currently there is no cure for HIV and AIDS but there are some drugs that slow down the action of the virus. The virus is present in blood and semen and is transmitted most commonly through sexual activity and by blood to blood contact. Although a wide range of people can become infected with HIV there are certain groups in society who have a higher risk of acquiring this infection, including homosexual and bisexual men, intravenous drug users and people who have several sexual partners. Once someone is diagnosed with HIV they have the virus for life and are aware that they are likely to die from an infection. People who are bereaved through HIV may have experienced several bereavements as they may be part of a group in society where many of their friends and acquaintances are living and have died with this virus.

The two characteristics of AIDS that may contribute to grief reactions are the period of anticipation of death for the person with AIDS and their family and friends and the unpredictable speed of the progression of this disease which is extremely variable.

A study into the grief reactions of those bereaved through HIV found that for many there was a stigma attached to dying as a result of this condition. Some of those grieving felt they were viewed by others as being flawed in some way by having a link with the person dying from HIV (Houck, 2007). This study also reported that some of those bereaved told others the person had died of some other cause in order to avoid this stigma. A need identified for the bereaved was for practitioners supporting them to recognize and acknowledge their grief, to make it 'enfranchised' by providing a safe and accepting environment where the bereaved person is able to express their thoughts, emotions and personal stories without fear of being judged. If the bereaved person has HIV themselves they may be concerned at how long they have left to live and how they may die. Groups consisting of others who have been bereaved of friends or family members with HIV can be helpful in giving and receiving support and sharing their experiences (Leaver et al., 2008). The death of many members of a community can result in the bereaved person grieving not just for the individuals who have died but for their community in terms of it being part of their identity and where they belong. Perreault et al. (2010) suggest that bereavement work in this situation should focus on the community and help people to develop and maintain strong peer networks and support groups.

Dementia

Alzheimer's disease and other types of dementia can result in multiple losses for both the person with the condition and for their family and friends (Doka, 2010).

For the person with dementia they may experier ʳ grid at the point of diagnosis concerning the memories ʳᵉ unable to recall and the knowledge that their memc continue to deteriorate further. They may find it d know that they used to be able to recall certain now unable to do so. They may no longer reme whom they were very close and knew over m

Applied example

Phil was very close to his uncle Bill, whom he had lived with for several years as a child. When Bill developed Alzheimer's he no longer remembered who Phil was and referred to him as 'this gentleman'. Phil found this very distressing and eventually decided not to visit his uncle any more as he found it too upsetting to experience him not recognizing who he was.

If a family member or close friend of the person with dementia dies they may not be able to remember that this has happened. They may ask where the person is and after being told they have died, become distressed and upset as if they have heard the news for the first time. This can be very distressing for families and carers and they should be reassured that this type of response is not uncommon. Some people with dementia may not respond to news of a death by being upset or they may confuse the person who has died with someone else. If a brother or sister has died they may think it is a parent who has died. A loss of their cognitive ability does not mean they do not experience emotions and a person's grief may be apparent through changes in behaviour such as agitation, anxiety or aggression (Rando, 1993). Supporting a person with dementia following a significant death requires much flexibility on the part of the practitioner. It is important to discover what will be helpful to that particular person at that specific time. It could be to offer support by being present, listening to the person and if appropriate the use of touch. Showing a photograph of the person to identify who it is and encouraging them to talk of the person may be useful, but at others times it could be helpful to deflect the issue and engage the person in other activities or conversation (Doka, 2010). The expression of grief by someone with dementia can be influenced by a range of factors including the stage of the disease, their ability to recognize and express the loss and their awareness of the significance of their relationship with the person who has died. It is important to validate the expressions of grief articulated by the person with dementia and support them with empathetic listening and responses.

For family and friends of the person with dementia there can be many issues around bereavement both before and after the person has died. There may be a loss experienced of the person they knew as the disease progresses resulting in family members not recognizing the behaviour and attitudes displayed by their partner, parent, sibling or other relative. The person's personality can seem so different to that which it had been that relatives may feel they have already experienced the death of the person they knew (Doka, 2002). Others will state clearly that the person they know so well is still there and that they can see glimmers of the personality and characteristics they always had. It can be distressing for relatives to experience bizarre behaviours from their loved one or for the person to be aggressive or speak in language they have never used before, expressing extreme socially unacceptable views. As the person with dementia becomes more dependent a spouse or other relative may become a full-time carer, leaving their job and becoming isolated as their caring role prevents them meeting others. This can result in the loss of important social networks and support systems for the carer, they may not recognize these losses until they have happened.

Applied example

Mary had spent the past three years caring for her husband Stan at home. She had gradually withdrawn from contact with friends and neighbours she used to meet regularly, she didn't have the time or the opportunity to go out and socialize. After Stan died she sat at home and did not dare contact her previous friends as she felt she had abandoned them for so long. Following encouragement from her local practice nurse she did contact a neighbour and was immediately invited round. This gave her confidence to contact others and re-engage with her local community.

The death of the person with dementia can result in very mixed emotions for the carer and other family members. There may be a sense of relief from their caregiving duties and an end to the suffering of their loved one, but this may be combined with guilt for having these feelings. Disenfranchised grief can occur if others do not recognize the grief experienced by some following the death. Some people may think the person had already died in that they were not able to recognize or engage with others and therefore the physical death is not significant. This lack of recognition can be very distressing for those grieving and may add to their feelings of guilt. Another loss following the death of a person with dementia can be the loss of their role as caregiver, the carer may feel they have lost their identity and not know what to do with their time as it was all taken previously in caring for their relative.

In supporting a person following the death of a person with dementia these multiple losses and possible responses need to be considered. The person may be supported to explore their varying responses and the changes in their life both when the person was alive and now they have died. Discussing the support systems they may have can be a useful activity. They may have lost touch with people they were close to in the past due to their caring role and encouraging them to re-establish connections and build up links again can be very beneficial for the bereaved person.

Conclusion

There are a range of deaths that are unrecognized or unacknowledged that can cause added distress and uncertainty to people already grieving. Helping people to recognize the loss they have experienced and how this may be expressed by people who may not have the words to verbally express it, can be useful to both the bereaved and their carers and relatives. Some may feel they should not be grieving as the person was not a close relative but a client or patient at work, or a colleague. Anyone we have a relationship with whether a personal friendship or a professional relationship can result in feelings of grief if that person dies. It is important to acknowledge and care for ourselves at this time.

Key points

Disenfranchised grief is grief that is not recognized, acknowledged or socially validated either by the person experiencing the bereavement or by others around them.

Assumptions can be wrongly made regarding people with learning disabilities and their ability to understand death and express their grief.

With HIV/AIDS there are often multiple losses experienced by people belonging to certain social and community groups.

In dementia there can be multiple losses both before and after the person with the condition dies.

Further Reading

Doka, K. (2002) *Disenfranchised Grief. New Directions, Challenges and Strategies for Practice.* Champaign, IL: Research Press.

Doka, K. (2010) Grief, Multiple loss and Dementia. *Bereavement Care,* 29(3), 15–20.

Houck, J. (2007) A Comparison of Grief Reactions in Cancer, HIV/ AIDS and Suicide Bereavement. *Journal of HIV/AIDS & Social Services,* 6(3), 97–112.

Oswin, M. (1991) *Am I Allowed to Cry? A Study of Bereavement amongst People who have Learning Difficulties.* London: Souvenir Press.

9 Self-care When Working with the Bereaved

Introduction

This final chapter covers the very important topic of self-care for the practitioner working with the bereaved. A major feature of this type of work is the emotional impact it has on the practitioner. Being able successfully manage these feelings is essential for all those working with the bereaved. In order to relate to the bereaved person, the practitioner becomes emotionally engaged with them and as a result can be left carrying emotions that they can find distressing. This engagement is referred to as emotional labour (Smith, 2012) and emotional intelligence needs to be developed by practitioners in order to manage these feelings in a healthy and constructive way. This chapter explores the negative effects that can develop in this type of work, coping strategies and defence mechanisms and aspects that may influence a practitioner's response. It concludes with positive strategies and structures that can be put in place to help a person manage their emotions in a constructive and positive manner

Emotional labour

Emotional labour involves practitioners acting out behaviours in order to convey to others their care and concern. These are commonly what Rogers (2002) refers to as the core conditions of empathy, unconditional positive regard and congruence. For practitioners working with the bereaved this can involve smiling and talking in a calming voice even though they may be anxious or worried (Smith, 2008). It is used to make clients feel safe and this feature has been identified as being particularly required when practitioners support people in stressful situations such as following the death of someone close to them (Smith, 2012). A study conducted in the 1990s (Smith, 1992) demonstrated the importance of emotional labour in nursing and that it produced emotional responses in others such as gratitude and feelings of safety and security. The use of emotional labour by practitioners can result in them being at risk of developing certain conditions including burnout and compassion fatigue.

Burnout

Burnout is a condition that can happen to health and social care practitioners over a period of time, which may be several years. It consists of physical, emotional and mental exhaustion, resulting from involvement in emotionally demanding situations over a long period of time (Beck, 2011). A characteristic of burnout concerns the demands felt by staff and the expectations of the organization where they work. This can lead to practitioners working long hours and trying to persevere in giving a high-quality of care with limited resources (Aycock and Boyle, 2008). It can result in them being unable to emotionally engage with the people they are supporting and can also affect their relationships outside of work. They may feel unable to be involved in social activities or to express emotional responses to those around them. They are likely to have difficulty concentrating both at work and home and feel continuously tired and exhausted. People who choose to work in health and social care are generally those who care about people and want to offer and provide a high level of support to the clients with whom they work. This can be achieved sometimes at the expense of the individuals own emotional and physical health. They may neglect their own needs for care and support in order to be available for others.

Compassion fatigue

The term compassion fatigue was first used by Joinson (1992) to describe how nurses can lose the ability to be caring with patients, however, it is also applicable to other practitioners in health and social care and voluntary organizations supporting those who are bereaved. Several environmental factors are identified as leading to this condition: expanding workloads, long hours, complex needs of clients and emotional distress. The resulting emotions seen in practitioners are tiredness, depression, anger, apathy and detachment.

Applied example

Emma worked in a centre for adults with long-term complex conditions caring for clients and supporting relatives. She had worked there for six years and in that time had experienced the death of several of the clients she had grown to know well. Recently she was aware that she always felt tired and irritable, which was unlike her. She was also conscious that when she met new clients, she was reluctant to engage with them or their family as she was concerned about the distress she would feel when they died.

A definition of this condition is a severe malaise resulting from caring for clients who are suffering and distressed (Sabo, 2006). Research into this issue by Hooper et al. (2010) concluded that warning signs of compassion fatigue often go unrecognized by practitioners themselves. This can result in them no longer having the emotional energy to care for themselves as well as becoming withdrawn from relating to their clients.

Vicarious trauma

Vicarious trauma is a term used to describe effects that can occur when a person is told about a traumatic event. It is not the result of experiencing a traumatic event for themselves but of listening to someone else relating their experience of trauma. It is also known as secondary traumatization (Rothschild, 2006). It is a condition that many practitioners supporting bereaved clients are very aware of as it can occur as they listen to client's stories, which can contain disturbing and upsetting situations. As the practitioner listens and supports the bereaved person in telling their story, the client has the opportunity to let go of some of their burden and to release some of their pain. The practitioner can have a stress reaction of being traumatized themselves by listening to the story. The practitioner may develop pictures in their mind or intense feelings running through their body. These symptoms may occur at the time the story is being told or could develop later that day or in subsequent days.

Applied example

Lynn volunteered with a bereavement charity and was supporting a client whose friend had died through suicide. The friend had gone missing and the client, along with others, went searching for him. It was the client who found his friend, sat in his car, having used the exhaust fumes piped into the car to effect his suicide. The client had opened the car door and touched his friend's face. The client gave a very detailed description of how his friend looked and how his skin felt. That evening the practitioner found she was imagining for herself what the person in the car looked like and found it difficult to detach from these thoughts and the picture she had created in her head. Over the next few days her thoughts kept returning to this incident.

For people who work with those who have experienced a traumatic event, it is important to acknowledge that there will be times when what they hear will have an adverse effect on them. These incidents can take the practitioner by surprise and they may be shocked at their strong emotional response to a situation. Recognizing that it is normal to be affected by this type of work and realizing that you are not alone in this is important. It is okay to feel outraged, horrified, shocked, saddened or vulnerable at what you may hear. Some practitioners feel they should always be able to manage their emotions themselves and that by experiencing vicarious trauma it somehow indicates that they are not competent in their role. On the contrary, hearing about trauma does affect a person and it would be of more concern if a practitioner was not affected at all by hearing distressing stories from their clients.

Coping with and managing the feelings and reactions to a client's trauma is an essential skill for those working in the area of bereavement. People deal with crises and trauma in different ways. Some of the ways are healthy and productive, such as having support networks of people to talk to, and other ways can be unhealthy and unproductive such as withdrawing from others and refusing to discuss what has happened. Workers need to be able to recognize their own warning signs and know what actions to take. This involves developing emotional intelligence, which enables the development of strategies and systems to care for themselves and seek out appropriate support.

Emotional intelligence

Emotional intelligence is discrete from academic ability and involves a number of aspects. It includes an individual being self-aware, able to recognize and manage personal emotions and having insight into how they relate to others (McQueen, 2003). Mayer and Salovey (1997) described emotional intelligence as the ability of a person to accurately perceive, evaluate and express emotions, and also to regulate their emotions in a way that promotes both emotional and intellectual growth.

Within nursing and other types of health and social care work, emotional intelligence is a feature that has been identified as being essential for this work. Whyte (1997) wrote that the nurse who is emotionally intelligent is one who can work in harmony with both their thoughts and their feelings and Freshwater and Stickley (2004) consider that emotional intelligence is fundamental to the act of caring. Cadmen and Brewer (2001) contend that the ability of a health or social care practitioner to manage their own emotions while interpreting and responding to those of others is a prerequisite of anyone working in the caring professions.

A related concept is that of self-compassion, the ability of a practitioner to recognize their own suffering and to care for themselves in a non-judgemental way. It has been recognized that those who have a good level of emotional intelligence along with self-compassion have a high level of mental and emotional wellbeing. Other studies have demonstrated that health and social care practitioners with high levels of emotional intelligence experienced lower levels of somatic illness and burnout when confronted with stressful situations (Mikolajczak et al., 2007). It has been found that emotional intelligence is not something that is fixed but can be increased by the person developing constructive coping strategies. These can include utilizing social support networks, taking exercise and talking to others (Birks et al., 2009). Those with low emotional intelligence have been found not to use social support networks and were more likely to engage in destructive or harmful behaviours when stressed such as eating more, drinking alcohol and smoking, and blamed factors outside their control for not being able to manage their time well and their disorganization. In a study of student nurses, those with high levels of emotional intelligence were found to have high levels of perceived competency and lower levels of stress (Por et al., 2010).

Coping strategies

The term coping strategies has been used to encompass coping and defence mechanisms. Coping mechanisms are conscious ways of trying to adapt to stress and anxiety that can be positive or negative, and defence mechanisms involve the individual protecting themselves from negative emotions (Gross, 2005).

There are a range of coping mechanisms that practitioners may use in relation to trying to manage emotional responses to their work. Emotional detachment is a technique comprising of withdrawal from emotional contact with others, and maintaining clear boundaries in relationships. It involves the mental disengagement from work, and of not thinking about or engaging in any work related activities once you leave your place of work (Sonnentag, 2012). It does not include a detached attitude towards work, and a study by Binnewies et al. (2010) found that employees who successfully detached from their work at the weekend were more proactive and had higher levels of job performance during the week. Other advantages of emotional detachment were identified as higher levels of psychological wellbeing, feeling more content and cheerful, and lower levels of psychosomatic symptoms, particularly in jobs with high stress levels.

Ways in which staff may actively detach from their work include talking to family members about their working day when initially home from work before moving on to other subjects, engaging in a hobby or other activity that requires their full attention and developing rituals, which they can use to help them detach as they travel home from work. A lack of such detachment has been found to lead to emotional exhaustion and burnout, along with a lowered performance at work (Maslach et al., 2001).

Other coping strategies involve building resilience through positive emotions (Pipe et al., 2011). The development of positive and optimistic responses to situations can build personal resources over time, enabling the individual to think creatively and address challenges. The repeated practice of responding positively to situations can lead to resilience in the individual and a positive impact on others (Frederickson and Losada, 2005).

It is suggested in several studies that humour has a positive relationship with feelings of wellbeing, and that laughing with friends or watching an amusing play or television programme can help the practitioner cope with their stress and anxiety. McCreaddie and Wiggins (2007) suggest that there is a positive connection between humour and health in their review of the function of humour in healthcare. Humour is identified as a stress moderator, which can result in the development of a positive emotional state and improve relationships amongst colleagues (Francis et al., 1999).

Defence mechanisms have been identified as being used by health and social care practitioners to reduce and manage levels of stress and anxiety in their working environment.
Some of these mechanisms include adhering to set procedures, consulting with colleagues and asking them to make decisions with them so they do not take sole responsibility. Another defence mechanism used is adhering to set practices with which the practitioner is familiar and avoiding any changes in their work routine. This feature was identified by Krantz (2010) in relation to information technologies that result in the speeding

up of work and reduce time for practitioners to reflect on their work.

Features affecting practitioner responses to their work

Practitioners bring their life experiences to their work and these can impact in a positive or negative way on their ability to perform their work.

Practitioners working with the bereaved will have times when there are traumas and difficult situations in their own personal lives. Any situation, in their personal life, which the person finds emotionally distressing is going to impact on how emotionally available they are to support clients. Personal circumstances that could be stressful involve: difficulties with relationships, illness of those close to them, financial problems or other family crises. The practitioner needs to be particularly vigilant at these times in looking after themselves and restricting their work to what they can manage emotionally and physically. They may need to take time away from their work or reduce the amount of people they support.

When a practitioner working with the bereaved experiences the death of someone close to them personally, they need to take time away from their work in order to grieve and process their own responses to the death. Some organizations have set time periods when people are not allowed to work with the bereaved following a personal bereavement. This could cover a wide range of time periods and is often from one to six months. Working with bereavement, when the practitioner is recently bereaved, could trigger strong emotions and add extra stress and trauma to the practitioner. The importance of support networks, self-awareness and support from managers are vital in this situation in order that the right decisions are made for the individual concerned.

When supporting a bereaved person the practitioner may be affected by the type of death being spoken of. They may find it triggers thoughts of someone close to them, for example, if it is someone of a similar age or type of death.

Applied example

Sue's mother was diagnosed with chronic heart failure and has had several admissions to hospital. Sue began supporting Emma whose mother had died of heart failure. Emma's mother was a similar age to Sue's and Sue struggled to keep focussing on Emma and not think about her own mother as Emma described how her mother had died.

If the practitioner has experienced trauma or death in their own life and have utilized successful coping strategies this may help them in supporting others following a death. However, if certain strategies have worked well for a practitioner personally they may try to persuade others to use the same techniques. Every person is an individual and what may be helpful to one person may not be to another. The practitioner needs to be aware of this and not assume that the client has a certain response or that set techniques will be beneficial to them.

Pressures of work can impact how a practitioner is able to perform their role. It may be only part of their role to support the bereaved and there may be not enough time for them to carry out this role adequately with the other tasks they have to do. There may be limited time available to offer support or they may only be able to see a bereaved person for a set number of sessions. This could result in the practitioner feeling they have not given the level or amount of support they would like to give and that they have somehow failed or have not been good enough.

Self-care strategies and systems

As a result of the emotionally demanding nature of working with bereavement, practitioners involved in this area of work need to cultivate activities that help them to relax, manage their emotions and restore their energy. It can take a variety of forms and can be very varied. The same activity may help one person to relax but could be an added source of stress to someone else. Many people utilize a range of activities and there follows some examples of the types of activities that may help people to manage their stress and improve their emotional wellbeing.

Supervision

Some practitioners have a formal system of supervision, which is part of their professional practice. Supervision involves meeting individually or in a group with a senior or experienced colleague to discuss issues that have arisen when working with the bereaved. In counselling and psychotherapy this is a formal arrangement and a requirement of the registration bodies of these professions. Other practitioners such as midwives and social workers also have supervision as a requirement of their professional practice. In some other health and social care settings clinical supervision is recommended but is not a compulsory requirement (Hawkins and Shohet, 2012). Many practitioners develop their own system for supervision with colleagues or peers. Peer supervision is where colleagues meet together to discuss issues from their work and support each other. This can be meetings between two people or in small groups. Supervision can be a formal arrangement where practitioners meet regularly, at set intervals such as monthly or can be more flexible. In order for supervision to be effective, the people involved need to feel comfortable with each other and be able to talk freely about what concerns them. They need to agree on issues such as confidentiality and practical issues such as the venue and length of the meeting. The supervisor may be from the same discipline as the practitioner or a different one, and they may be within the organization or from outside it. A supervisor should not be the line manager of the practitioner as this could lead to unclear boundaries and the practitioner not feeling able to share certain concerns. There may be issues within the organization the practitioner may want to discuss but feels unable to talk about these directly to their line manager. The ideal is for the practitioner to choose their own supervisor who they can relate well to and can trust (Shohet 2007).

Social support

Talking to people, whether in a formal supervision setting or informally with colleagues is a self-care strategy identified as being beneficial by many health and social care practitioners (Wilson and Kirshbaum, 2011). Most practitioners in this field work as part of a team and colleagues can be an important source of support. This can take a range of forms including: listening to the person who is stressed, empathizing with them and encouraging them with compliments and positive feedback. This activity was recognized as being beneficial by Hochschild (1983) in her study of flight attendants. She identified a feature she called 'collective emotional labour' where flight attendants worked as part of a team helping each other in boosting morale and giving support when one of them had a challenging experience with a passenger or some other stressful situation. This support took the form of banter, listening to the person who was stressed, empathizing with them and encouraging them with compliments and positive feedback. This resulted in the staff becoming close and intimate with each other and helped them to work as a cohesive team.

An activity that is often combined with talking is that of drinking tea. This may seem an insignificant action, however, there is research to demonstrate that drinking tea can actually lower stress levels and results in people feeling cared for and valued. Cross and Michaels (2009) conducted research into the social and psychological effects of tea consumption on stress. The research consisted of two groups of 21 people whose stress levels were measured before and after being given stress inducing tasks to complete. Following the tasks and before having their stress levels tested for the second time, one group was given tea to drink and the second group was given glasses of water.

The findings showed that both groups had no significant differences in their stress levels before the stress inducing tasks; however, the tea drinking group showed a 25 per cent reduction in stress levels at the conclusion of the experiment. In focus groups following the experiment, the tea drinking participants stated that the making and consuming of tea made a significant contribution to moderating their stress. They reported feeling relaxed when drinking tea and observed that this activity enabled them to draw a line under their stressful experience and that they used tea as a coping mechanism to help deal with other stresses in their lives. They also reported that the act of making tea resulted in them feeling cared for and having a sense of communality with others in their group. It helped them to build a rapport with each other and engage in conversation. In contrast the water drinking group drank in silence. These findings are supported by de Beauvoir's work (1972) that identified tea drinking as a ritual associated with feelings of communality and solidarity. Williams and Bargh (2008) suggest that the positive effects of tea include behaviour related to feelings of interpersonal warmth and trustworthiness that by holding a cup of warm tea people perceive those around them as possessing a warmer personality and of being more caring. Cross and Michaels (2009) also suggest that making and drinking tea was a core aspect of British culture, and that the social and psychological aspects of this ritual enhance its effects on both our bodies and our brains.

Humour

A strategy used in stressful situations by some health and social care practitioners is banter and humour. It has been found that humour can contribute to a sense of community and be a means of mutual support for practitioners (Kinsman and Major, 2008) Humour is identified as a stress moderator, which can result in the development of a positive emotional state and improve relationships amongst staff (Francis et al., 1999). This is supported by Abel (2002) who suggests that humour is used by nurses to help them cope with a job that involves a high percentage of emotional labour and stressors such as caring for people who are dying. Although humour can be helpful it needs to be used appropriately and with sensitivity.

Physical activity

Taking part in physical activity has been found to help people to relax, reduce levels of stress and helps people feel energized (Mollart et al., 2011).

It can take a variety of forms and can be competitive or social. For some engaging in competitive sport such as tennis, badminton, football or hockey can be an outlet for emotional energy and there is usually a social aspect attached to belonging to a club or team. Others may prefer a more solitary form of activity, for example, walking, running, cycling or lane swimming though these activities can be done as part of a group as well. Physical activity has been shown to be beneficial for mental health, memory function and can reverse the negative effects of stress (Head et al., 2012).

Mindfulness and relaxation techniques

Mindfulness is increasingly being recognized as being a form of self-care that can be helpful to those working in the caring professions (Newsome et al., 2013). It involves the practitioner developing an awareness of the present moment without judgement and not ruminating about anxieties of the past or the future. It also helps practitioners to be aware and attentive to their own needs as well as those of others (Rothschild, 2006). Findings from research into the use of mindfulness in the work setting have found that as participants develop skills in recognizing their own self-care needs and being accepting and compassionate to themselves they were able to extend these qualities to others at work, both colleagues and clients (Newsome et al., 2013).

Yoga, Tai Chi and other relaxation techniques such as breathing exercises have been found to have significant health benefits and to reduce stress levels (Huang et al., 2013, Yadav et al., 2012). Guided imagery and relaxation techniques have been shown to result in stress reduction for staff and can result in enhanced performance (Boehm and Tse, 2013)

Other activities

Some people benefit from engaging in an activity very different from their work and find their relaxation in a hobby such as needlework, woodworking or other crafts. It has been found that an activity that requires great concentration such as model building or working with an engine can help a person to detach from thoughts of their work as the activity requires their full attention (Maslach et al., 2001) Others may engage in a range of activities such as gardening, motorcycling or cooking.

Group activities such as community singing groups have been found to improve resilience and the quality of life for those involved (Sun et al., 2012). Some may prefer other relaxing activities such as watching a film, listening to music, visiting a place of interest or the theatre. What may be beneficial for some could cause added stress for others.

Applied example

Jane: I love going lane swimming when I have had a stressful day, I just swim up and down the pool and find it really helps me to relax and switch off from work.

Pat: Swimming results in me feeling more stressed, I find it such a pressure, particularly when the pool is busy. My idea of a relaxing evening is going to watch a film.

An essential feature of self-care is for each individual to find what works for them, and then make sure they engage in activities that help them relax. Sometimes when a person is very busy and under stress they do not engage in these activities because of lack of time or of being too tired. It is when a person feels under pressure that it is important to engage in relaxing activities, as not doing so could lead to more stress and may even result in the practitioner having to have time off from their work.

Conclusion

For those working with the bereaved, competent self-care is crucial. It is a strength rather than a weakness to admit that in certain circumstances extra support is needed or time away from this type of work is required. Supporting the bereaved is a costly activity in terms of emotional energy and in order to be able to provide a high standard of support to others, self-awareness and self-care are essential. It is also very rewarding and satisfying work. To initially meet someone who is feeling very sad and not seeing any point in life and then to watch them as they re-engage with life, develop their social networks and move forward with plans and hopes for their future is extremely rewarding and encouraging.

Key points

Working with bereavement involves emotional labour and practitioners need to develop emotional intelligence in order to recognize and manage their emotional responses to this work.

Practitioners can be at risk of developing burnout, compassion fatigue and suffering from vicarious trauma.

There may be situations in a practitioner's personal life or other factors that can affect their ability at work.

Regular supervision, whether formal or informal can be a very beneficial way to care for yourself.

There are a range of self-care strategies and systems that can be useful to individuals, it is important to find out what works for you.

Further Reading

Hawkins, P. and Shohet, R. (2012) *Supervision in the Helping Professions*, 4th edn. Milton Keynes: Open University Press.
Rothschild, B. (2006) *Help for the Helper: The Psychophysiology of Compassion Fatigue and Vicarious Trauma*. New York: W. W. Norton and Company.

Sources of Information and Support

Australia

Australian Centre for Grief and Bereavement
Provides education, counselling, research and clinical services
for those working in and affected by experiences of grief and
bereavement
http://www.grief.org.au

Bereavement Care Centre
Provides comprehensive and accessible counselling and
support services to the terminally ill and their families and for
those recently bereaved
http://www.bereavementcare.com.au/

Grief Link
Information resources for those bereaved and grieving, their
carers, friends and colleagues and for health and welfare
workers
http://www.grieflink.asn.au

Lifeline
Support for those bereaved by suicide
http://www.lifeline.org.au

National Association for Loss and Grief
Offers grief support groups, training and advice on grief
issues
http://www.nalag.org.au

The Compassionate Friends
Offers friendship and understanding to bereaved parents,

siblings and grandparents who are grieving the death a child of any age, from any cause
http://tcfaustralia.org.au

The White Wreath Association
Offers support to those bereaved by suicide
http://www.whitewreath.com

New Zealand

Grief Centre
Provides support, advice and counselling to those affected by loss and grief
http://www.griefcentre.org.nz

Skylight
Support for people of all ages facing tough life situations of change, loss, trauma or grief
http://www.skylight.org.nz

United Kingdom

Bereavement UK
Information about death, dying, funerals and self help
http://www.bereavement.co.uk

Brake
Road safety charity, supporting those affected by road traffic collisions
http://www.brake.org.uk

Child Bereavement Charity
Support for families and professionals when a child dies
http://www.childbereavement.org.uk/

The Compassionate Friends
Support for bereaved parents and their families
http:// www.tcf.org.uk

Cruse Bereavement Care
Support, information and advice for the bereaved
http://www.cruse.org.uk

Miscarriage Association
Support and information on pregnancy loss
http://www.miscarriageassociation.org.uk

SAMM
Support for those bereaved by murder, manslaughter or
unlawful killing.
http://www.samm.org.uk

SANDS
Support for parents bereaved by stillbirth or neonatal death
http://www.sands.org

SCARD
Support and care after road death and injury
http://www.scard.org.uk

Survivors of Bereavement by Suicide (SOBS)
Support groups for anyone affected by suicide
http://www.sobs.admin.care4free.net

UK Funerals online
Information relating to funerals
http://www.UK-funerals.co.uk

Way Foundation
National support group for those widowed under 50yrs of age
http://www.wayfoundation.org.uk

United States of America

GriefShare
Local grief support groups specifically for those grieving the
death of a loved one
http://www.griefshare.org

MISS Foundation
International organization providing support to grieving
families, and reducing infant and toddler death through
research and education
http://www.misschildren.org

SHARE Organization (National)
Support groups and newsletters for bereaved parents, their
family and friends
http://www.nationalshare.org

The Compassionate Friends
Supports families following the death of a child of any age
and provides information to help others be supportive
http://compassionatefriends.org

UNITE
An organization in Philadelphia providing grief support
services to families suffering from miscarriage, stillborn,
ectopic and neonatal loss
http://www.unitegriefsupport.org

References

Abel, M. (2002) Humour, stress and coping strategies. *Humor: International Journal of Humor Studies*, 15(4), 365–81.

Abeles, M. and Samson, J. (2010) A time to mourn: Reflections on Jewish bereavement practices. *Bereavement Care*, 29(1), 19–22.

Addicott, R. and Ross, S. (2010) *Implementing the End of Life Care Strategy: Lessons for Good Practice* (London: Kings Fund).

American Psychiatric Association (2013) *Diagnostic and Statistical Manual of Mental Disorders V* (Washington: American Psychiatric Publishing).

Asaro, R. (2001) Working with adult homicide survivors, part II: Helping family members cope with murder. *Perspectives in Psychiatric Care*, 37(4), 115–25.

Aycock, N. and Boyle, D. (2008) Interventions to manage compassion fatigue in oncology nursing. *Clinical Journal of Oncology Nursing*, 13(2), 183–91.

Beck, C. (2011) Secondary traumatic stress in nurses: A systematic review. *Archives of Psychiatric Nursing*, 25(1), 1–10.

Bento, R. (1994) When the show must go on. Disenfranchised grief in organizations. *Journal of Managerial Psychology*, 9(6), 35–44.

Binnewies, C., Sonnentag, S. and Mojza, E. (2010) Recovery during the weekend and fluctuations in weekly job performance: a week-level study examining intra-individual relationships. *Journal of Occupational and Organizational Psychology*, 83, 419–41.

Birks, Y., McKendree, J. and Watt, I. (2009) Emotional intelligence and perceived stress in healthcare students: A multi-institutional, multi-professional survey. *BMC Medical Education* 9(61): 61–68.

Boehm, L., and Tse, A. (2013) Application of guided imagery to facilitate the transition of new graduate Registered Nurses. *The Journal of Continuing Education in Nursing*, 44(3) 113–19.

Bonanno, G. (2009) *The Other Side of Sadness: What the New Science of Bereavement Tells Us about Life after Loss* (New York: Basic Books).

Bowlby, J. (1980) *Attachment and Loss Volume 3; Loss Sadness and Depression* (London: Hogarth Press).

Cadmen, C. and Brewer, J (2001) Emotional intelligence: A vital pre-requisite for recruitment in nursing. *Journal of Nursing Management*, 9(6), 321–24.

Cawkhill, P. (2009) Death in the armed forces. Casualty notification and bereavement support in the UK military. *Bereavement Care*, 28(2), 25–30.

Children's Act (2004) Available at: http://www.legislation.gov.uk/ukpga/2004/31/contents

Churchill, A. and Tay, C. (2008) An assessment of roadside memorial policy and road safety. *Canadian Journal of Transportation*, 2(1), 2–12.

Clarke, J. (2013) *Spiritual Care in Everyday Nursing Practice* (Basingstoke: Palgrave Macmillan).

Clayton, P., Desmarais, L. and Winokur, G. (1968) A study of normal bereavement. *American Journal of Psychiatry*, 125, 168–78.

Cross, M. and Michaels, R. (2009) The social psychological effects of tea consumption on stress, City University of London.

Crown Prosecution Service (2012) *Homicide: Murder and Manslaughter: Legal Guidance*. Available at: http://www.cps.gov.uk

Currier, J., Holland, J. and Neimeyer, R. (2006) Sense-making, grief, and the experience of violent loss: Towards a meditational model. *Death Studies*, 30, 403–28.

Currier, J., Neimeyer, R. and Berman, J (2008) The effectiveness of psychotherapeutic interventions for bereaved persons: a comprehensive quantitative review. *Psychological Bulletin*, 134, 648–61.

Davis, R. and Pless, B. (2001) BMJ bans 'accidents': Accidents are not unpredictable. *British Medical Journal*, 322, 1320–1.

De Beauvoir, S. (1972) *The Coming of Age* (New York: W. W. Norton).

Doka, K. (2002) *Disenfranchised Grief, New Directions, Challenges, and strategies for Practice* (Champaign, IL: Research Press).

Doka, K. (2010) Grief, multiple loss and dementia. *Bereavement Care*, 29(3), 15–20.

Donnelly, E. and Neville, L. (2008) *Communication and Interpersonal Skills* (Exeter: Reflect Press).

Egan, G (2013) *The Skilled Helper*, 10th edn (Elmont, Brookes/Cole Groups).

Elwart, F. and Christakis, N. (2008) The effect of widowhood on mortality by the causes of death of both spouses. *American Journal of Public Health*, 98(11), 2092–8.

Eriksson, I. and Nilsson, K. (2008) Preconditions needed for establishing a trusting relationship during health counselling – an interview study. *Journal of Clinical Nursing*, 17, 2352–9.

Evans, R. (2012) Emotional care for women who experience miscarriage. *Nursing Standard*, 26(42), 35–41.

Folta, J. and Deck, G. (1976) Grief the funeral and the friend. In V. Pine (ed.) *Acute Grief and the Funeral* (Springfield, IL: Charles C. Thomas).

Francis, L., Monahan, K. and Berger, C. (1999) A laughing matter: the uses of humour in medical interaction, *Motivation and Emotion*, 23(2), 155–74.

Fredrickson, B. and Losada, M. (2005) Positive affect and the complex dynamics of human flourishing. *American Psychologist*, 60(7), 678–86.

Freshwater, D. and Strickley, T. (2004) The heart of the art: Emotional intelligence in nurse education. *Nursing Inquiry*, 11(2), 91–98.

Freud, S. (1917) *Mourning and Melancholia* (London: Hogarth Press).

Freud, S. (1949) Mourning and melancholia. In Jones E. (ed.) *Sigmund Freud MD LLD Collected Papers*, Vol. 4 [original work published in 1917] (London , Hogarth Press).

Gelder, M., Mayou, R. and Geddes, J. (2005) *Psychiatry*, 3rd edn (Oxford: Oxford University Press).

Gilbert, M. and Orlans, V. (2011) *Integrative Therapy, 100 Key Points and Techniques* (Hove: Routledge).

Glaser, B. and Stauss, A. (1965) *Awareness of Dying* (Piscataway, NJ: Transaction Publishers).

Goleman, D. (1995) *Emotional Intelligence* (London: Bloomsbury Publishing).

Grisham, J. and Williams, A. (2009) Cognitive control of obsessional thoughts. *Behaviour, Research and Therapy*, 47, 395–402.

Groos, A. and Shakespeare-Finch, J. (2013) Positive experiences for participants in suicide bereavement groups: A grounded theory model. *Death Studies*, 37, 1–24.

Gross, R. (2005) *Psychology, The Science of Mind and Behaviour*, 5th edn (London: Hodder and Stoughton).

Handsley, S. (2001) 'But what about us?' The residual effects of sudden death on self-identity and family relationships. *Mortality*, 6(1), 9–29.

Hawkins, P. and Shohet, R. (2012) *Supervision in the Helping professions*, 4th edn (Milton Keynes: Open University Press).

Head, D., Singh, T. and Bugg, J. (2012) The moderating role of exercise on stress-related effects on the hippocampus and memory in later adulthood. *Neuropsychology*, 26(20), 133–43.

Herz-Brown, F. (1989) The impact of death and serious illness on the family life cycle. In Carter B. and McGoldrick M. (eds) *The Changing Family Life Cycle: A Framework for Family Therapy*, 2nd edn (Needham Heights: Allen and Bacon).

Hinduism Today (2007) Death and dying. The Hindu view of the grand departure and its sacred rites of passage. *Hinduism Today*, January/February/March, 1–6.

Hochschild, A. (1983) *The Managed Heart: Commercialization of Human Feeling* (Berkeley: University of California).

Holmes, J. (1993) *John Bowlby and Attachment Theory* (London: Routledge).

Hooper, C., Craig, J., Janvrin, D., Wetsel, M. and Reimels, E. (2010) Compassion satisfaction, burnout and compassion fatigue among emergency nurses compared with nurses in other selected inpatient specialities. *Journal of Emergency Nursing*, 36(5), 420–27.

Houck, J. (2007) A comparison of grief reactions in cancer, HIV/AIDS and suicide bereavement. *Journal of HIV/AIDS and Social Sciences*, 6(3), 97–112.

Huang, F., Chien, D. and Chung, U. (2013) Effects of Hatha Yoga on stress in middle aged women. *The Journal of Nursing Research*, 21(1), 59–66.

Hunt, M. and Hunt, B. (1977) *The Divorce Experience* (New York, McGraw-Hill).

Johnson, N., Backlund, E., Sorlie, P.D., Loveless, C.A. (2000) Marital status and mortality: The national longitudinal mortality study. *Annals of Epidemiology*, 10, 224–38.

Johnston, D. and Mayers, C. (2005) Spirituality: A review of how occupational therapists acknowledge, assess and meet spiritual needs. *British Journal of Occupational Therapy*, 68(9), 386–92.

Joiner, T. (2007) *Why People Die by Suicide* (Harvard: Harvard University Press).

Joinson, C. (1992) Coping with compassion fatigue. *Nursing*, 22(4), 118–20.

Kalma, C., Cooper, C. and Robertson, M. (2012) *Psychiatry at a Glance* (Chichester: Wiley).

Katz, R. and Johnson, T. (2006) *When Professionals Weep; Emotional and Countertransference Responses in End of Life Care* (New York: Routledge).

Keesee, N., Currier, J. and Neimeyer, R. (2008) Predictors of grief following the death of one's child: The contribution of finding meaning. *Journal of Clinical Psychology*, 64(10), 1145–63.

Kinsman, R. and Major, J. (2008) From critical care to comfort care: The sustaining value of humour. *Journal of Clinical Nursing*, 17, 1088–95.

Kirby, S., Hart, D., Cross, D. and Mitchell, G. (2004) *Mental Health Nursing* (Basingstoke: Palgrave Macmillan).

Kirshbaum, M. (2011) Talking about death and dying: Must we really? *British Journal of Community Nursing*, 16(4), 181.

Klass, D., Silverman, P.R. and Nickman, S. (1996) *Continuing Bonds: New Understandings of Grief* (London: Taylor & Francis).

Kohner, N. and Henley, A. (2001) *When a Baby Dies* (London: Routledge).

Krantz, J. (2010) Social defences and twenty-first century organisations. *British Journal of Psychotherapy*, 26(2), 192–200.

Kristensen, P., Weisaeth, L. and Heir, T. (2010) Predictors of complicated grief after a natural disaster: A population study two years after the 2004 south-east tsunami. *Death Studies*, 34, 137–50.

Kübler-Ross, E. (1973) *On Death and Dying* (London: Routledge).

Leaver, C., Perreault, Y. and Dematrakopoulos, A. (2008) Understanding AIDS-related bereavement and multiple loss among long-term survivors of HIV in Ontario. *The Canadian Journal of Human Sexuality*, 17(1–2), 37–52.

Lee, E. (2012) Complex contribution of combat-related post-traumatic stress disorder to veteran suicide: Facing an increasing challenge. *Perspectives in Psychiatric Care*, 48, 108–15.

Lewis, C. (1961) *A Grief Observed* (London: Faber and Faber).

Lindeman, E. (1944) Symptomatology and recovery from acute grief. *American Journal of Psychiatry*, 101, 141–8.

Lipp, A. (2009) Termination of pregnancy: A review of the psychological effects on women. *Nursing Times*, 105(1), 26–9.

Lundin, T. (1987) The stress of unexpected bereavement. *Stress Medicine*, 3: 109–14.

MacConville, U. (2010) Roadside memorials, making grief visible. *Bereavement Care*, 29(3), 34–6.

MacDonald, P. (2009) Supporting people who self-harm. *Practice Nurse*, 37(9), 31–2.

Malkinson, R. and Bar-tur, L. (2005) Long term bereavement processes of older parents: The three phases of grief. *Omega*, 50, 103–29.

Mandal, B., Wilkins, E., Dunbar, E. and Mayon-Whyte, R. (2004) *Lecture Notes on Infectious Diseases*, 6th edn (Oxford: Blackwell Publishing).

Maslach, C., Schaufeli, W. and Leiter, M. (2001) Job burnout. *Annual Review of Psychology*, 52, 397–422.

Mayer, J. and Salovey, P. (1997) What is emotional intelligence? In P. Salevoy and D. Sluyter (eds.) *Emotional Development and Emotional Intelligence* (New York: Basic Books).

McCabe, C. and Timmins, F. (2013) *Communication Skills for Nursing Practice*, 2nd edn (Basingstoke: Palgrave Macmillan).

McCreaddie, M. and Wiggins, S. (2007) The purpose of humour in health, healthcare and nursing: a narrative review. *Journal of Advanced Nursing*, 61(6), 584–95.

McCutcheon, L., Maltby, J., Houran, J. and Ashe, D. (2004) *Celebrity Worship: Inside the Minds of Stargazers* (Baltimore: Publish America).

McDonald, S., Magill-Cuerden, J. and Mayes, M. (2011) *Mayes Midwifery: A Textbook for Midwives*, 14th edn (London: Baillie re Tindall).

McQueen, A. (2003) Emotional intelligence in nursing work. *Journal of Advanced Nursing*, 47(1), 101–8.

Metzger, P. and Gray, M. (2008) End of life communication and adjustment: Pre-loss communication as a predictor of bereavement related outcomes. *Death Studies*, 32, 301–25.

Mikolajczak, M., Menil, C. and Luminet, O. (2007) Explaining the protective effect of trait emotional intelligence regarding occupational stress: Exploration of emotional labour processes. *Journal of Research in Personality*, 41, 1107–17.

Miller, B. and McGown, A. (1997) Bereavement: Theoretical perspectives and adaptation: Canberra, Australia. *The American Journal of Hospice and Palliative Care*, July/August, 156–77.

Mollart, L., Skinner, V., Newing, C. and Foureur, M. (2011) Factors that may influence midwives work-related stress and burnout. *Women and Birth*, 26, 26–32.

Moos, N. (1995) An Integrative model of grief, *Death Studies*, 19, 337–64.

National Council for Palliative Care (2008) *Dying Matters* (London: National Council for Palliative Care).

National End of Life Care Programme (2011) *Guidance for Staff responsible for Care after Death* (Norwich: HMSO).

Neimeyer, R. (2001) *Meaning, Reconstruction and Experience of Loss* (Washington, DC: American Psychological Association).

Neimeyer, R. (2010) Grief counselling and therapy. The case for humility. *Bereavement Care*, 29(1), 4–7.

Newman, M. (2009) Post-traumatic stress disorder. *Bereavement Care*, 28(1), 31–3.

Newsome, S., Waldo, M. and Gruszka, C. (2013) Mindfulness group work: preventing stress and increasing self-compassion among helping professionals in training. *Journal of Specialists in Group Work*, 37(4), 297–311.

Norris, F., Friedman, M. and Watson, P. (2002) Disaster victims speak: part 11. Summary and implications of the disaster mental health research. *Psychiatry*, 65(3), 240–60.

Office for National Statistics (2012) Mortality Statistics: Deaths Registered in England and Wales (Series DR), 2010, Available at: http://www.ons.gov.uk/ons/rel/vsob1/mortality-statistics-deaths-registered-in-england-and-wales-series-dr-/2010/index.html

Oswin, M. (1991) *Am I Allowed to Cry? A Study of Bereavement amongst People who have Learning Difficulties* (London: Souvenir Press).

Parker-Hall, S (2009) *Anger, Rage and Relationship* (Hove: Routledge).

Parkes, C. (1975) *Bereavement; Studies of Grief in Adult Life* (London Penguin).

Parkes, C. (1996) *Bereavement: Studies of Grief in Adult Life*, 3rd edn (London, Routledge).

Parliamentary and Health Services Ombudsman (2013) *The NHS Hospital Complaints System: A Case for Urgent Treatment* (London: Parliamentary and Health Service Ombudsman).

Payne, S., Seymour, J. and Ingleton, C. (2004) *Palliative Care Nursing: Principles and Evidence for Practice* (Maidenhead: Open University Press).

Payne, S., Seymour, J. and Ingleton, C. (2008) *Palliative Care Nursing: Principles and Evidence for Practice*, 2nd edn (Maidenhead, Open University Press).

Perreault, Y., Fitton, W. and McGovern, M. (2010) The presence of absence: Bereavement in long term survivors of multiple AIDS-related losses. *Bereavement Care*, 29(3), 26–33.

Pies, R (2013) Bereavement does not immunize against major depression. *Medscape*, 24 January, 1–3.

Pipe, T., Buchda, V., Launder, S., Hudak, B., Hulvey, L., Karns, K. and Pendergast, D. (2011) Building personal and professional resources of resilience and agility in the healthcare workplace. *Stress and Health*, 28, 11–22.

Pollack, C. (2003) Intentions of burial: Mourning, politics and memorials following the massacre at Srebrenica. *Death Studies*, 27, 125–42.

Por, J., Barriball, L., Fitzpatrick, J. and Roberts, J. (2010) Emotional intelligence: its relationship to stress, coping, well-being and professional performance in nursing students. *Nurse Education Today*, 31, 855–60.

Radford, S. and Bloch, P. (2012) Grief, commiseration and consumption following the death of a celebrity. *Journal of Consumer Culture*, 12(2), 137–55.

Rando, T. (1993) *Treatment of Complicated Mourning* (Champaign, IL: Research Press).

Rapley, M., Moncrieff, J. and Dillon, J. (2011) *De-Medicalising Misery, Psychiatry, Psychology and the Human Condition* (Basingstoke: Palgrave Macmillan).

Reid, D., Field, D., Payne, S. and Relf, M. (2006) Adult bereavement in five English hospices: Participants, organisations and pre-bereavement support. *International Journal of Palliative Nursing*, 12(7), 320–7.

Riches, G. and Dawson, P. (1998) Spoiled memories: Problems of grief resolution in families bereaved through murder. *Mortality*, 3(2), 143–59.

Rinpoche, A. (2013) *Main Points to Consider when a Buddhist Dies* (Dumfries: Buddhist Funeral Services).

Roberts, A. and McGilloway, S. (2010) Bereavement support in a hospice setting. *Bereavement Care*, 29(1), 14–18.

Rogers, C. (2002) *Client Centred Therapy* (London, Constable).

Rogers, C. (2003) *Client Centred Therapy: It's Current Practice, Implications and Theory* (London: Constable and Robinson).

Rollin, B. (1992) Divorce and grief: Some philosophical underpinnings. In A. Tieman, B. Danto and S. Gullo (eds) *Divorce Shock: Perspectives on Counselling and Therapy* (Philadelphia, PA: The Charles Press).

Rothschild, B. (2006) *Help for the Helper: The Psychophysiology of Compassion Fatigue and Vicarious Trauma* (New York: W. W. Norton and Company).

Sabo, B. (2006) Compassion fatigue and nursing work: can we accurately capture the consequences of caring work? *International Journal of Nursing Practice*, 12(3), 136–142.

Samaritans (2011) *Suicide Statistics Report 2011* (London: Samaritans).

Samaritans (2013) *Myths about Suicide*. Available at: http://www.samaritans.org/how-we-can-help-you/myths-about-suicide

Sandler, I., Wolchik, S. and Ayres, T. (2008) Resilience rather than recovery: A contextual framework for adaptation following bereavement. *Death Studies*, 32: 59–73.

Santino, J. (2001) *Signs of War and Peace* (Basingstoke: Palgrave Macmillan).

Sarhill, N., LeGrand, S., Islambouli, R., Davis, M. and Walsh, D. (2001) The terminally ill Muslim: Death and dying from the Muslim perspective. *American Journal of Hospice and Palliative Care*, 18(4), 251–5.

Schut, H., Stroebe M., van den Bout, J. and Terheggen, M. (2001) The efficacy of bereavement interventions: Determining who benefits. In M. Stroebe, R. Hansson, W. Stroebe and H. Schut (eds) *Handbook of Bereavement Research: Consequences, Coping and Care* (Washington, DC: American Psychological Association).

Scott, S. (2000) Grief reactions to the death of a divorced spouse revisited, *Omega*, 41(3), 207–19.

Shapiro, E. (2008) Whose recovery, of what? Relationships and environments promoting grief and growth. *Death Studies*, 32, 40–58.

Shohet, R. (2007) *Passionate Supervision* (London: Jessica Kingsley).

Smith, H. (2004) *Griefkeeping: Learning How Long Grief Lasts* (New York: Crossroad Publishing).

Smith, P. (1992) *The Emotional Labour of Nursing: How Nurses Care* (Basingstoke: Palgrave Macmillan).

Smith, P. (2008) Compassion and smiles: What's the evidence? *Journal of Research in Nursing*, 13(5), 367–70.

Smith, P. (2012) *The Emotional Labour of Nursing Revisited*, 2nd edn (Basingstoke: Palgrave Macmillan).

Sonnentag, S., Kuttler, I. and Fritz, C. (2010) Job stressors, emotional exhaustion and need for recovery: A multi-source study on the benefits of psychological detachment. *Journal of Vocational Behaviour*, 76, 355–65.

Stephenson, J. (1986) Grief of siblings. In T. Rando (ed.) *Parental Loss of a Child* (Champaign, IL: Research Press).

Stokes, J. (2009) Resilience and bereaved children. Helping a child to develop a resilient mind-set following the death of a parent. *Bereavement Care*, 28(1), 9–17.

Stroebe, M. (2002) Paving the way from early attachment theory to contemporary bereavement research. *Mortality*, 7(2), 127–38.

Stroebe, M. and Schut, H. (1998) Culture and grief. *Bereavement Care*, 17(1), 7–11.

Stroebe, M. and Schut, H. (1999) The dual process model of coping with bereavement: rationale and description. *Death Studies*, 23(3), 197–224.

Stroebe, M., Stroebe, W. and Hannson, W. (1993) *Handbook of Bereavement* (Cambridge: Cambridge University Press).

Sun, J., Buys, N. and Merrick, J. (2012) Mental health promotion via participatory community singing. *International Journal of Child and Adolescent Health*, 5(3), 217–18.

Szasz, T. (1974) *The Myth of Mental Illness: Foundations of a Theory of Personal Conduct*, rev. edn (New York: Harper Collins).

Taylor, S., Koch, W., Fecteau, G., Fedoroff, I., Thordarson, D. and Nicki, R. (2001) Post traumatic stress disorder arising after road traffic collisions: Patterns of response to cognitive-behaviour therapy. *Journal of Consulting and Clinical Psychology*, 69(3), 541–51.

Terrorism Act (2000) Available at: http://www.legislation.gov.uk/ukpga/2000/11/contents

Thompson, N. (2011) *Grief and its Challenges* (Basingstoke: Palgrave Macmillan).

Tompkins, O. (2010) Panic attacks. *American Association of Occupational Health Nurses Journal*, 58(6), 268.

Tugendhat, J. (2005) *Living with Loss and Grief* (London: Sheldon Press).

Wade, D., Nursery, J., Forbes, D. and Creamer, M. (2012) A multi-level framework to guide mental health response following a natural disaster. *Bereavement Care*, 31(3), 109–13.

Wakefield, J. (2013) DSM–5: An overview of changes and controversies. *Clinical Social Work Journal*, 41: 139–54.

Walker, J., Payne, S., Smith, P. and Jarrett, N. (2007) *Psychology for Nurses and the Caring Professions*, 3rd edn (Maidenhead: Open University Press).

Walter, T. (1999) *On Bereavement: The Culture of Grief* (Maidenhead: Oxford University Press).

Walter, T. (1996) A new model of grief: Bereavement and biography, *Mortality*, 1(1), 7–25.

Whyte, D. (1997) *The Heart Aroused: Poetry and the Preservation of the Soul at Work* (London: The Industrial Society).

Williams, L. and Bargh, J. (2008) Experiencing physical warmth promotes interpersonal warmth. *Science*, 322(5901), 606–7.

Wilson, J. and Kirshbaum, M. (2011) Effects of patient death on nursing staff: A literature review, *British Journal of Nursing*, 20(9), 559–63.

Wilson, R. (1992) Whirlpool of grief, lecture presented at the Child and Death International Conference, Edinburgh.

Woodroffe, I. (2013) Supporting bereaved families through neonatal death and beyond. *Seminars in Fetal and Neonatal Medicine*, 18, 99–104.

Worden, W. (2010) *Grief Counselling and Grief Therapy: A Handbook for the Mental Health Practitioner*, 4th edn (New York: Springer).

Wright, S. (2005) *Reflections on Spirituality and Health* (London: Whurr Publishers Ltd).

Yadav, R., Magan, D., Mehta, N., Sharma, R. and Mahapatra, S. (2012) Efficacy of a short-term yoga-based lifestyle intervention in reducing stress and inflammation: Preliminary results. *The Journal of Alternative and Complimentary Medicine*, 18(7), 662–7.

Index